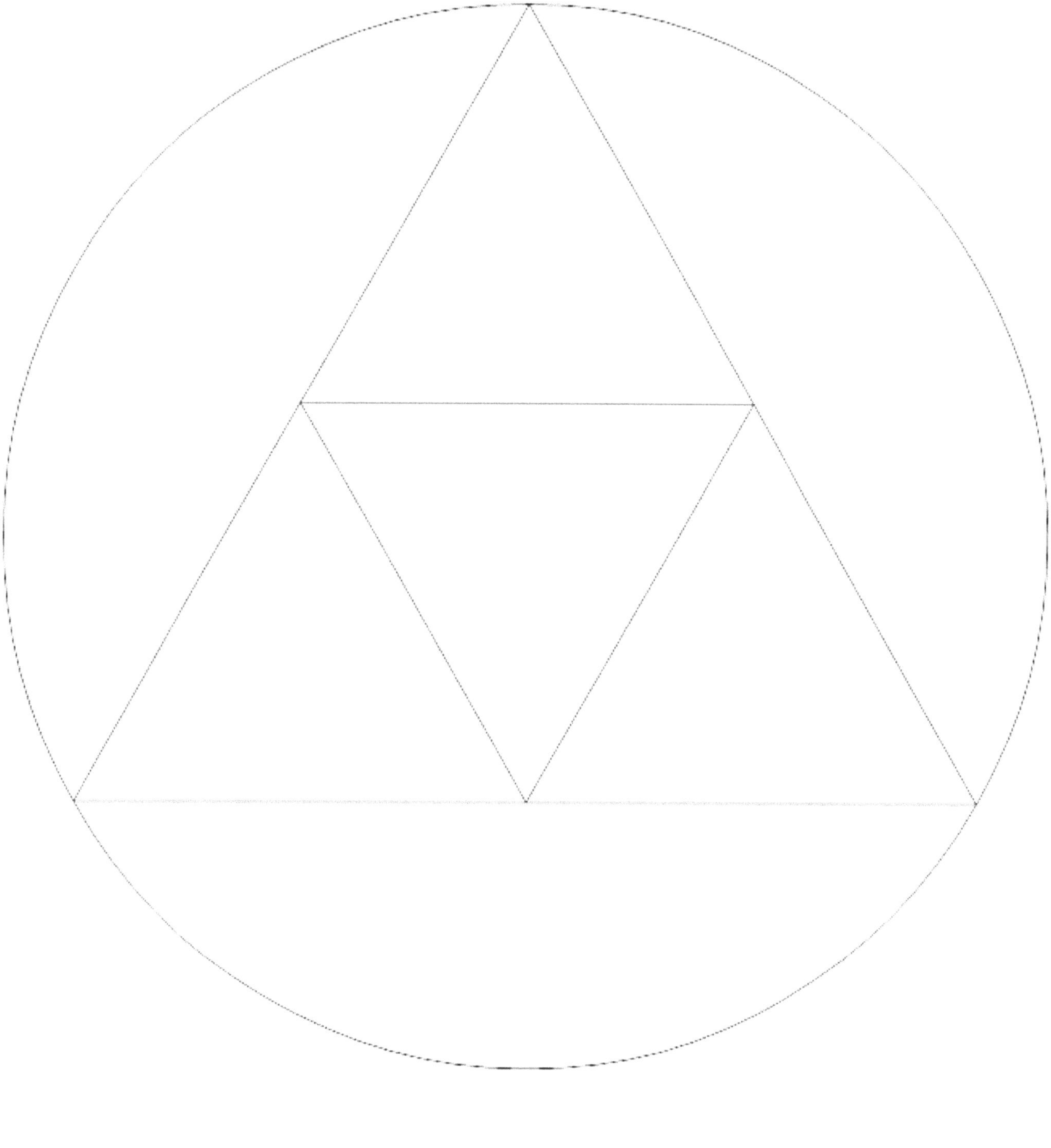

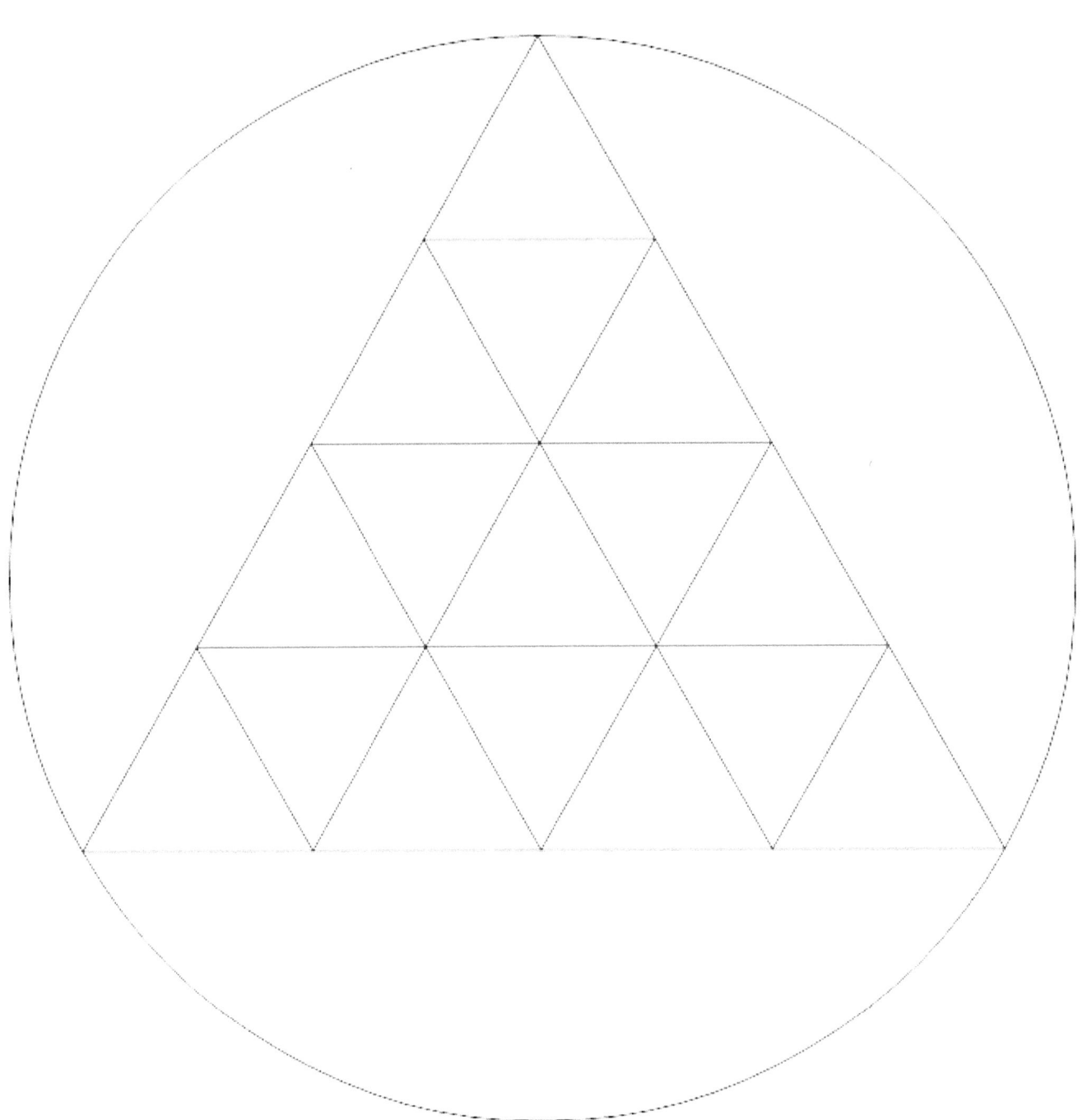

This is my very first coloring book. The idea is to simply have shape tessellations with black strokes so that anyone who buys this book can color them in any way they like. Because of this I don't even need to include titles since what happens in the end will be up to the users.

Also, circles will be a central theme because I like regular polygons and for this reason there will be regular polygons or tessellations of them inside a big circle on every page.

The main focus is on doing things with what I call the seven deadly shapes. The triangle, square, pentagon, hexagon, pentagram, hexagram, and circle. There are some good reasons why these are my favorite shapes.

The triangle, square, pentagon, hexagon are the first four regular polygons and also are unique in that they tessellate perfectly with each other. However, the pentagon only tessellates in three dimensional space and the hexagon only in two dimensional space. For this reason there won't be pure pentagon tessellations in a book but I can do some other funny things with them as you will soon see.

I included some of my other existing designs but modified them so that they have only black strokes and no fill colors.

The following pages contain all new designs I made for the first time for this book specifically. In the future I may add more pages to this book even after it's published if I have anything really good to add. For the time being though, I wanted to get it out so people can enjoy coloring what I have so far.

It's also possible for me to digitally color most of these in a similar way that people might do with pencils and markers. If you come up with your own colors that you would like to have printed on a variety of products, I can help make it happen. Check out my Society6 store here.

https://society6.com/chandlerklebs

And email me at : chandlerklebs@gmail.com if you have any special requests of art you'd like done or want me to make something else part of future art books or my store on Society6.

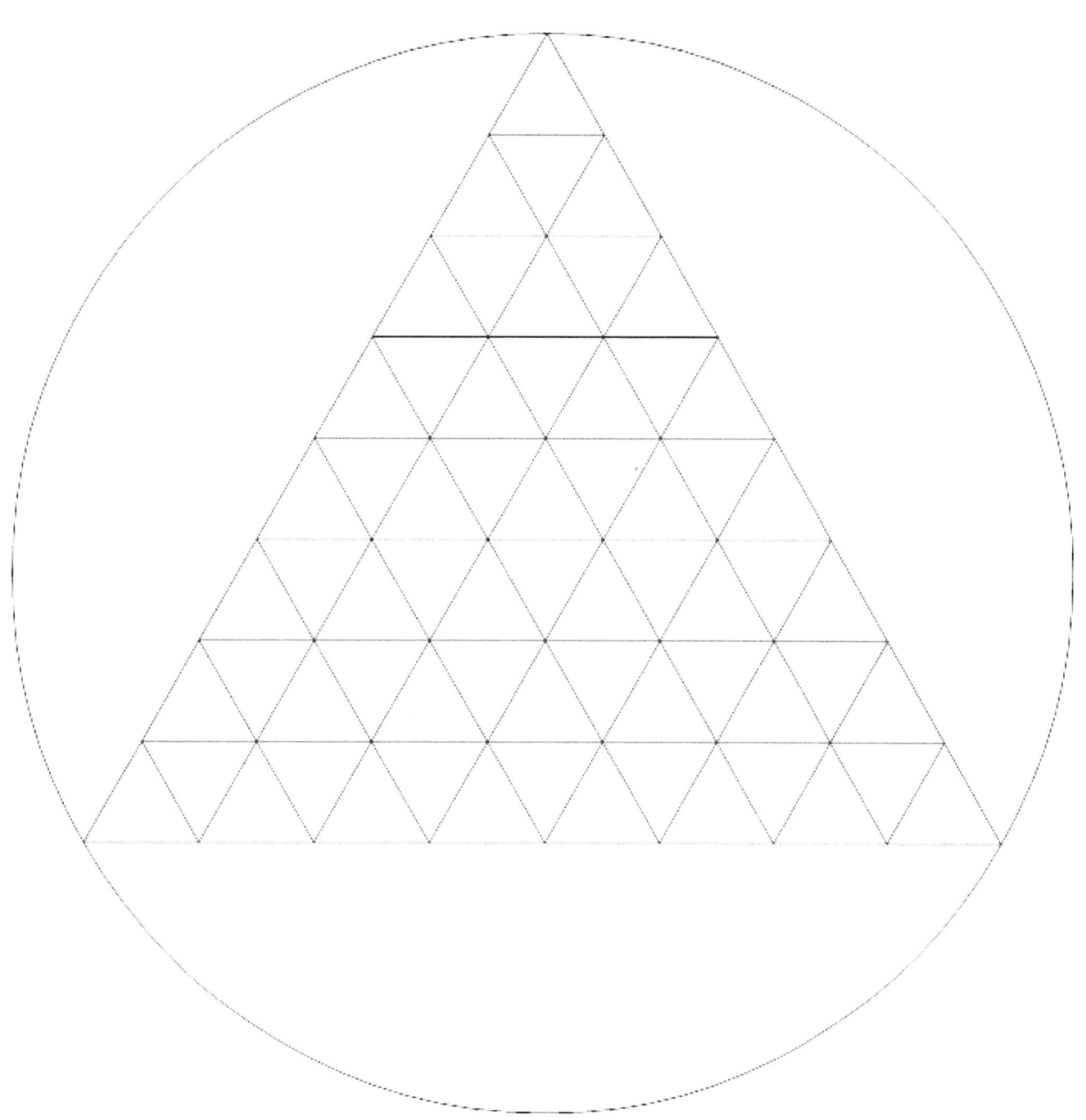

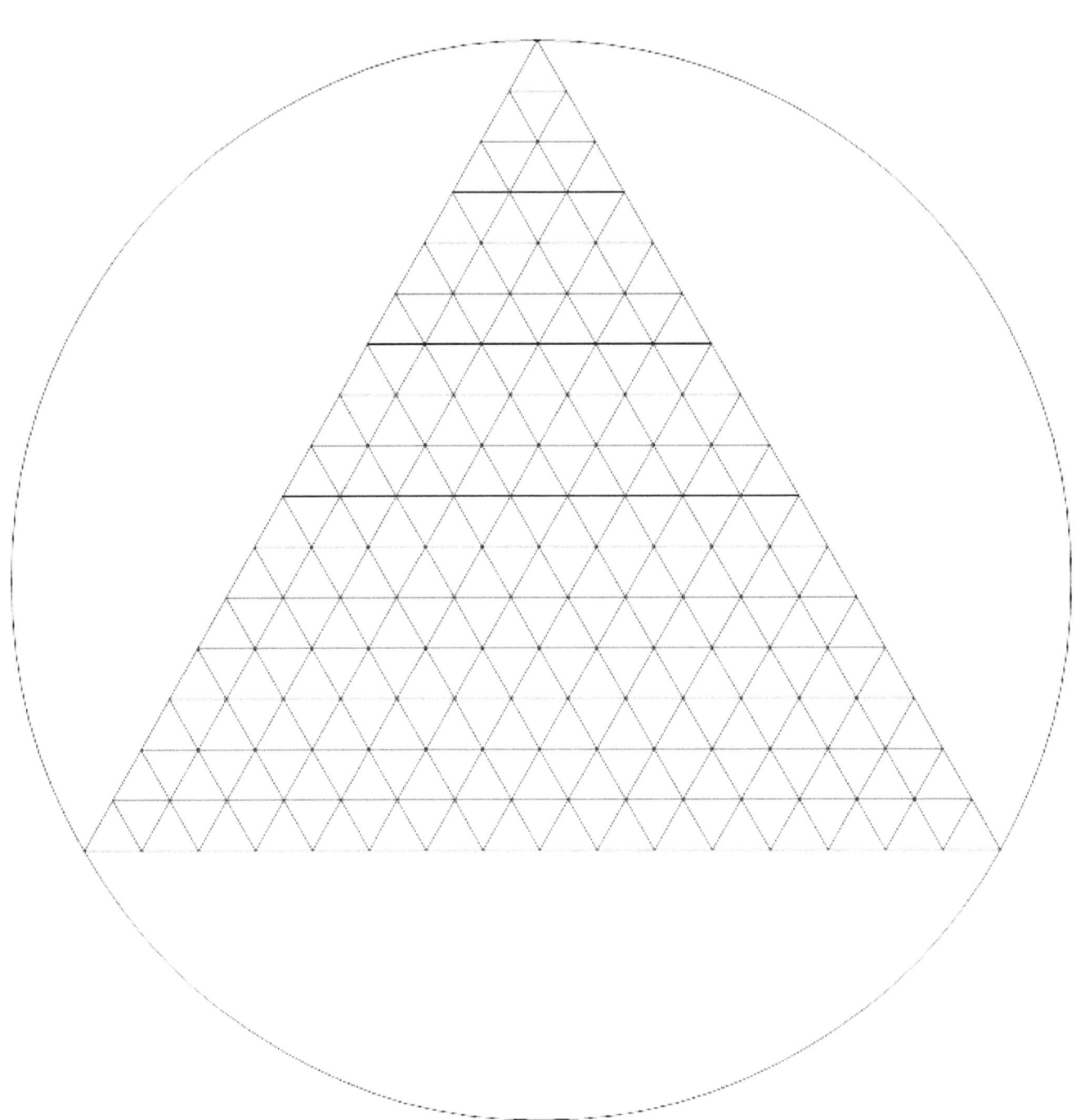

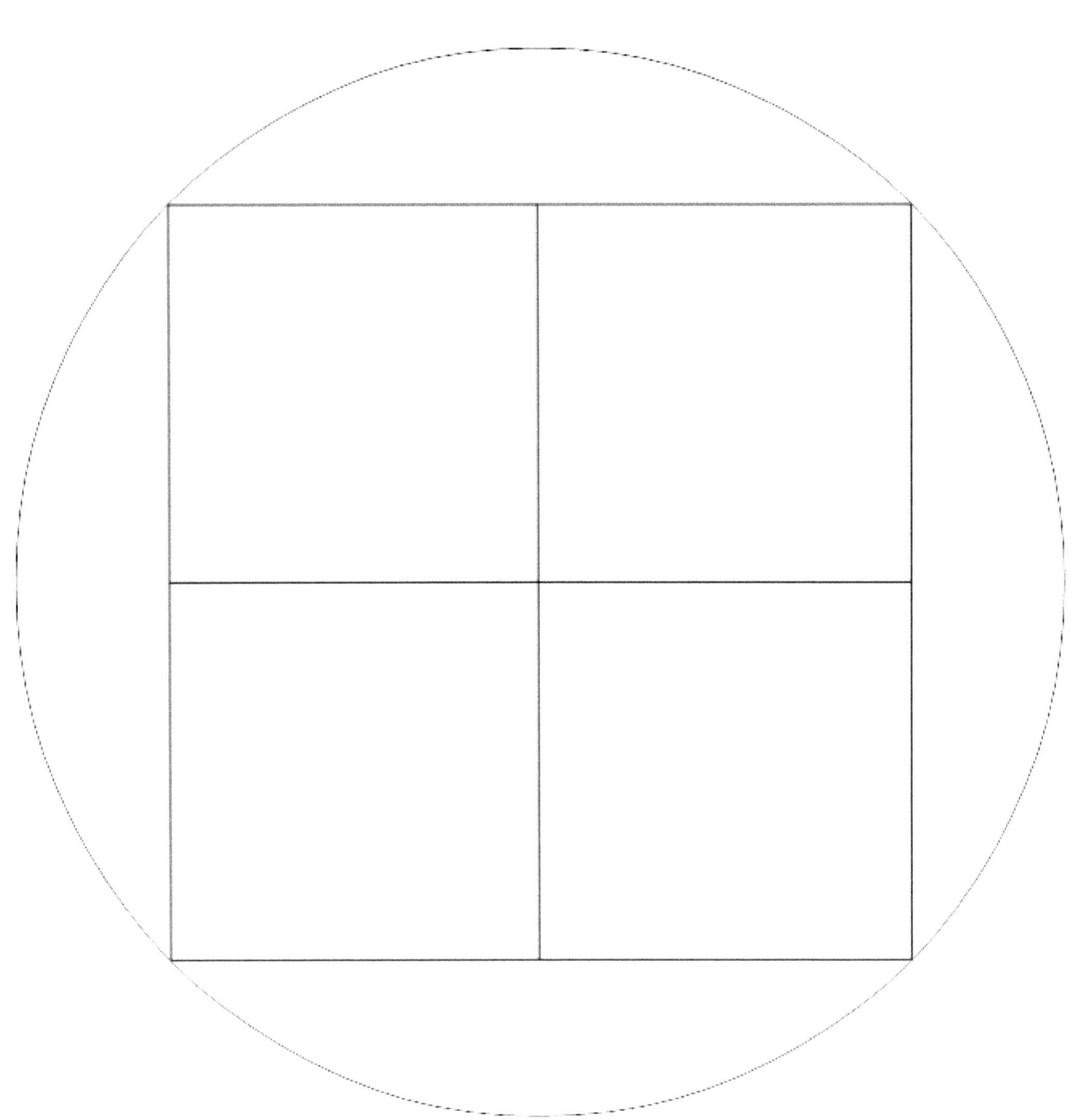

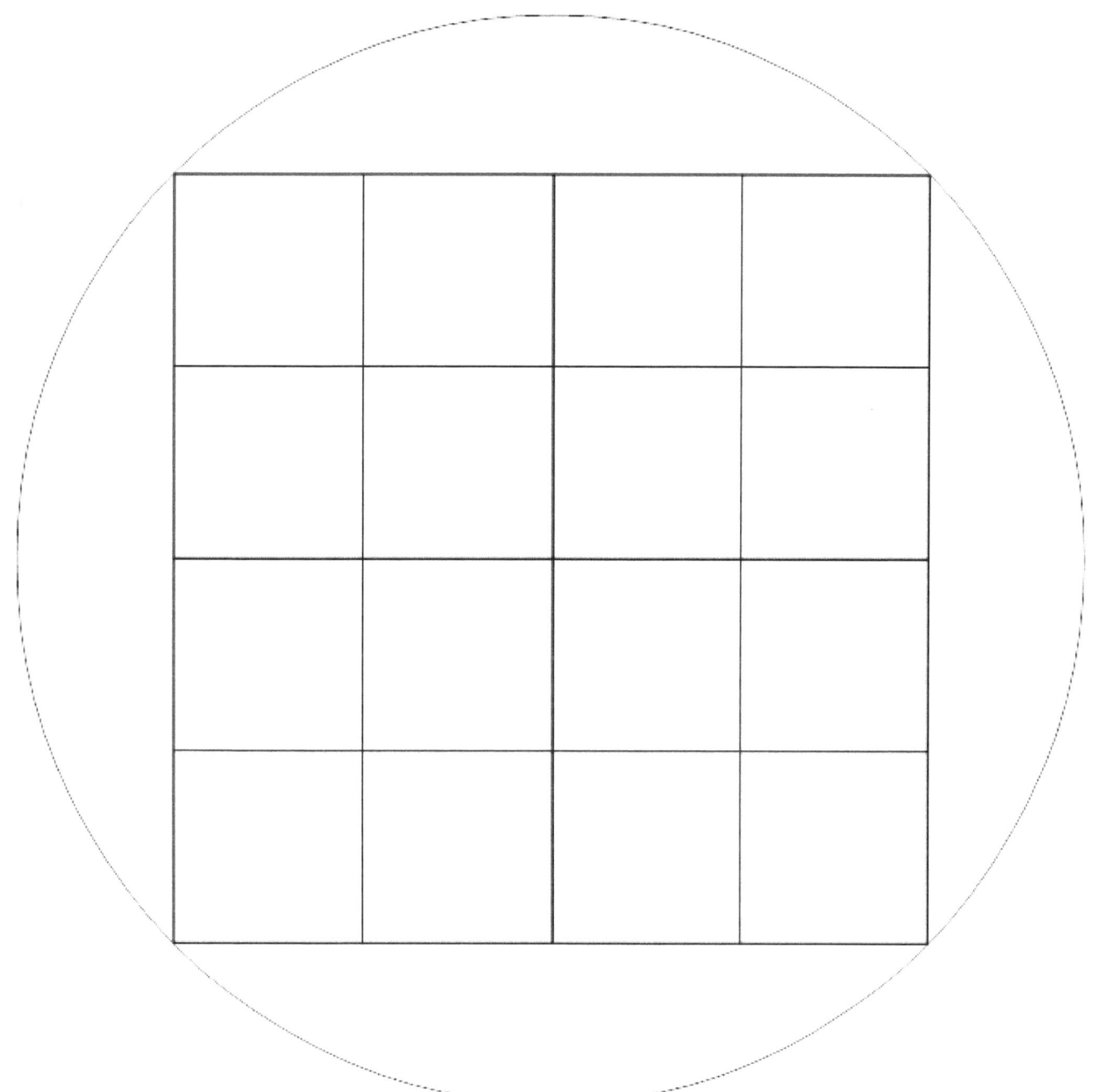

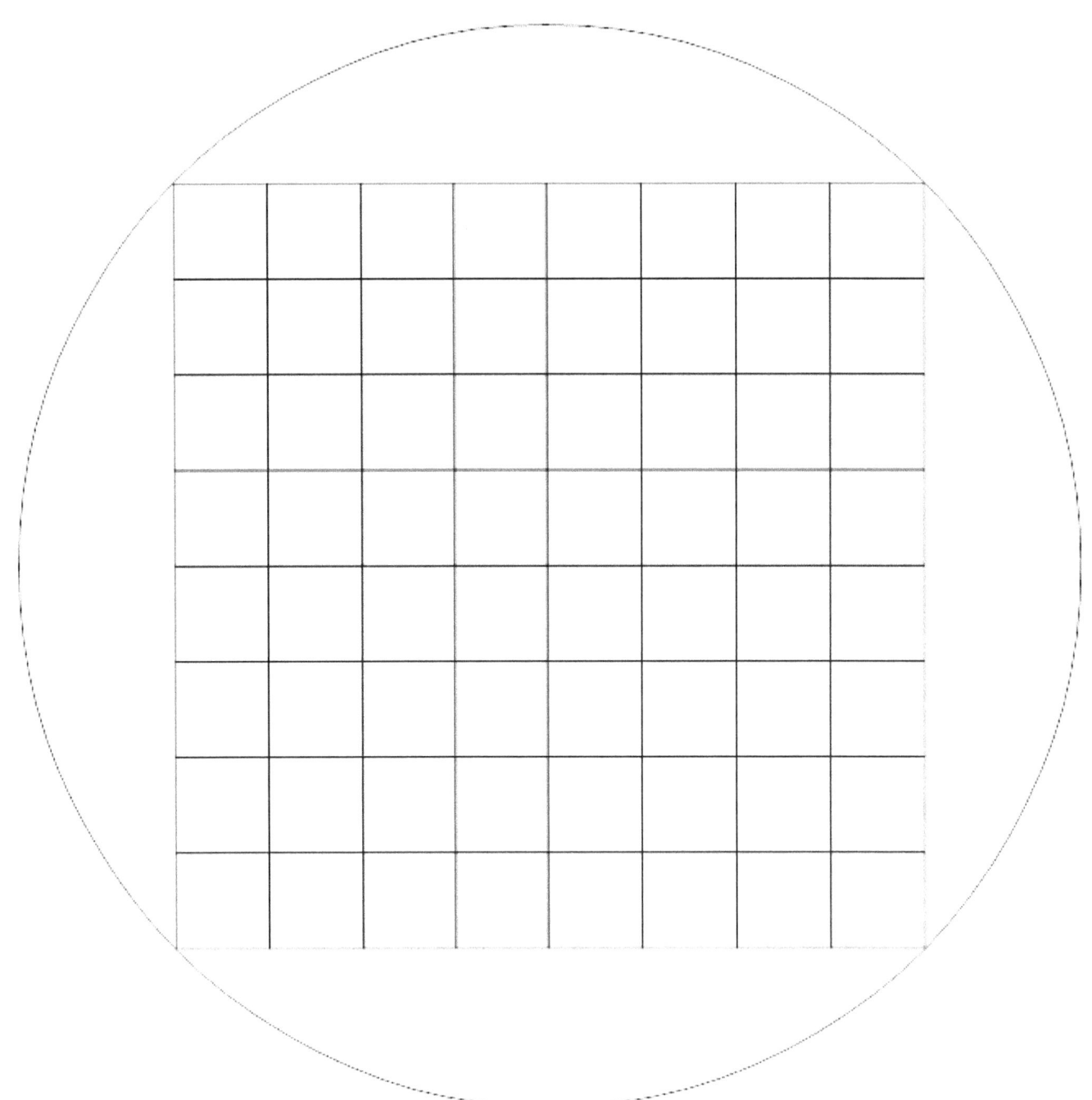

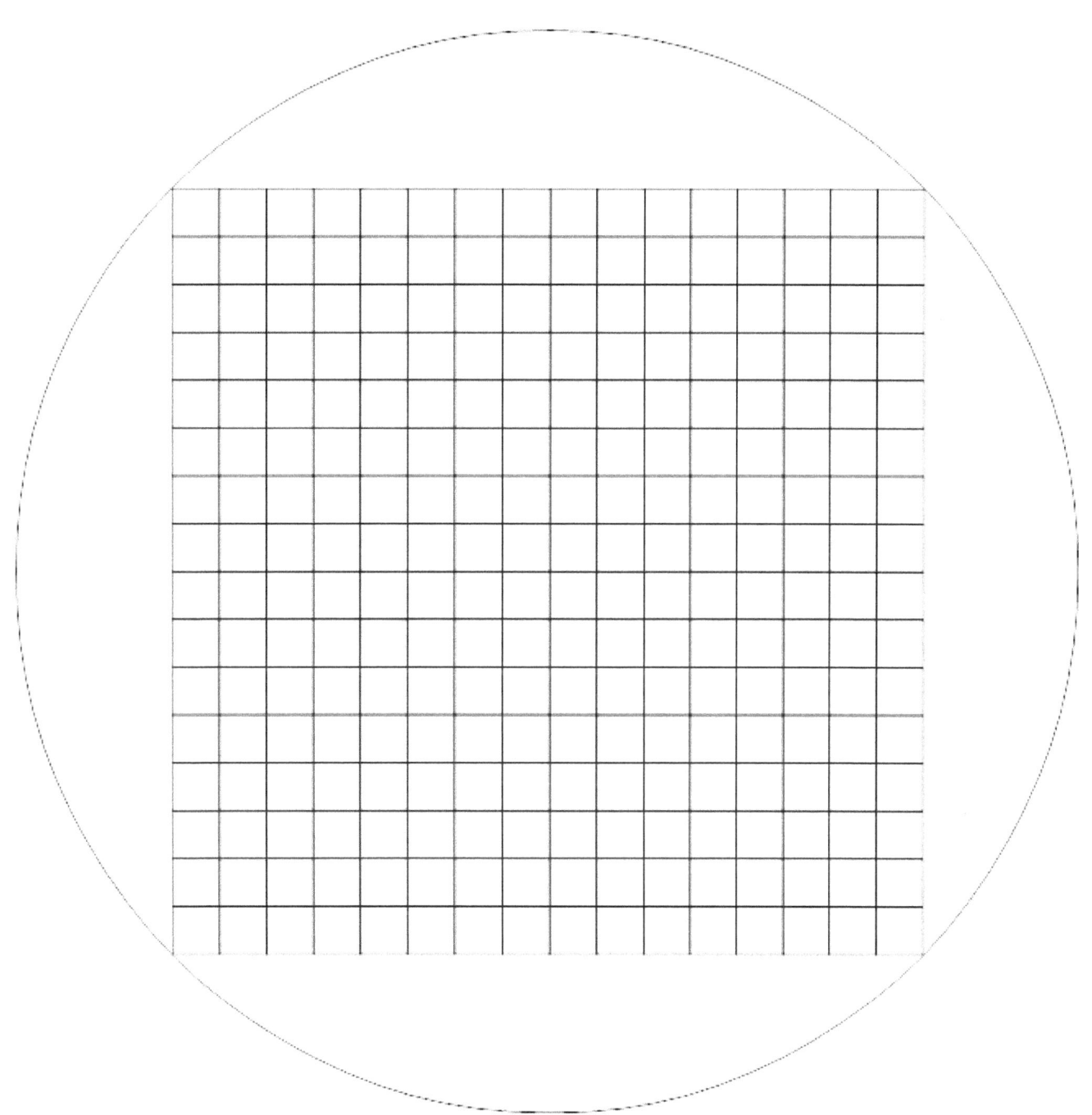

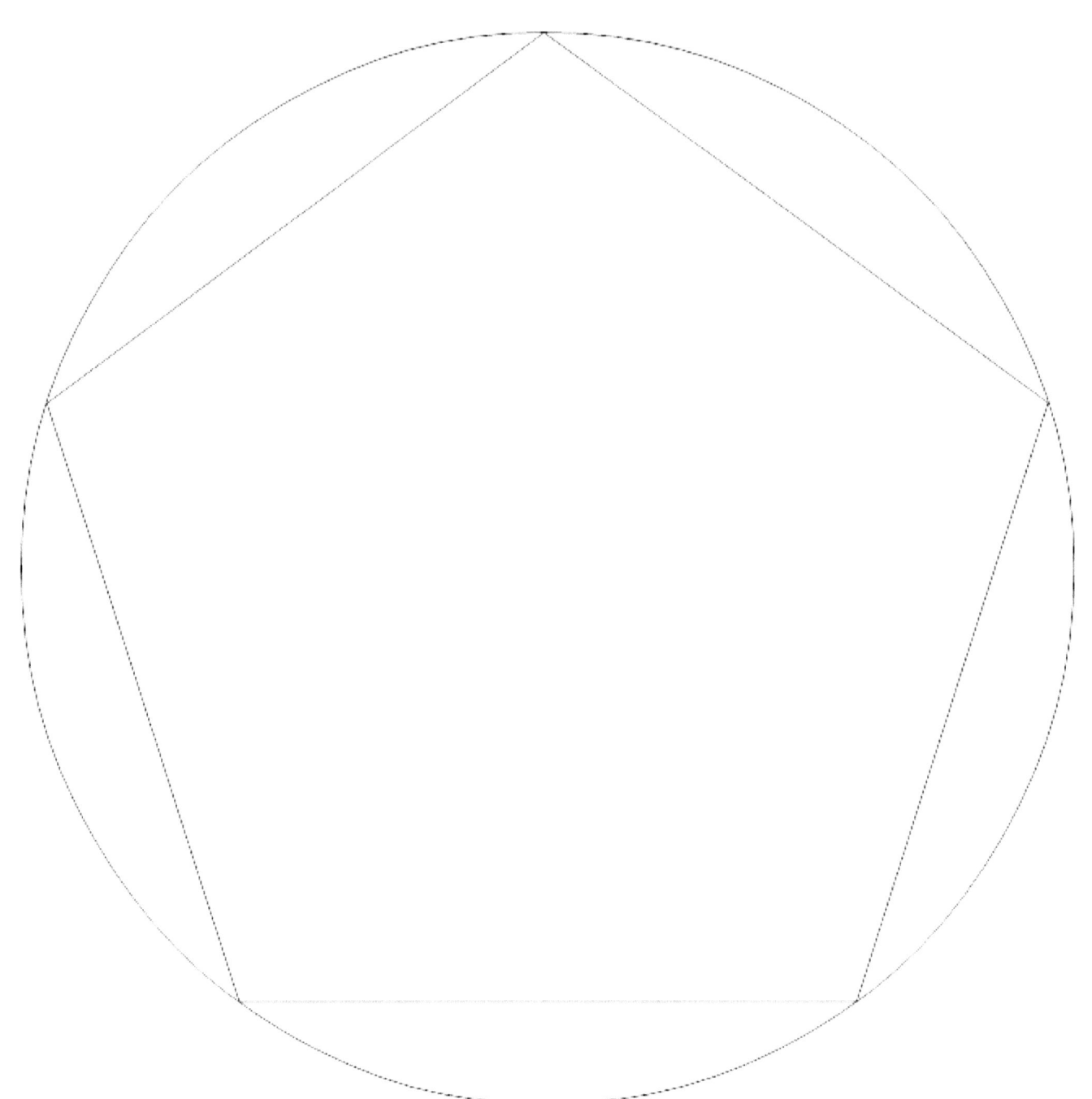

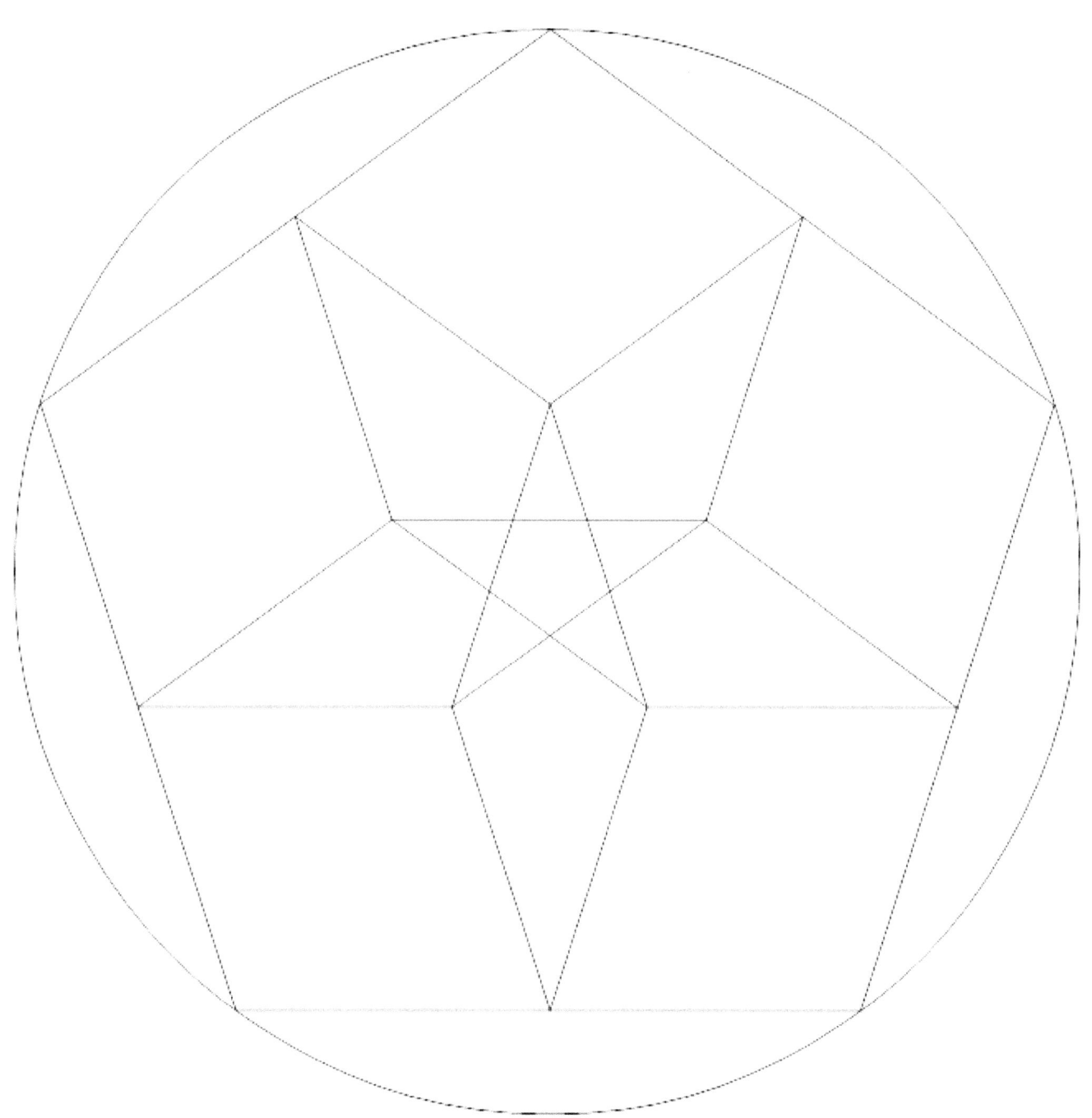

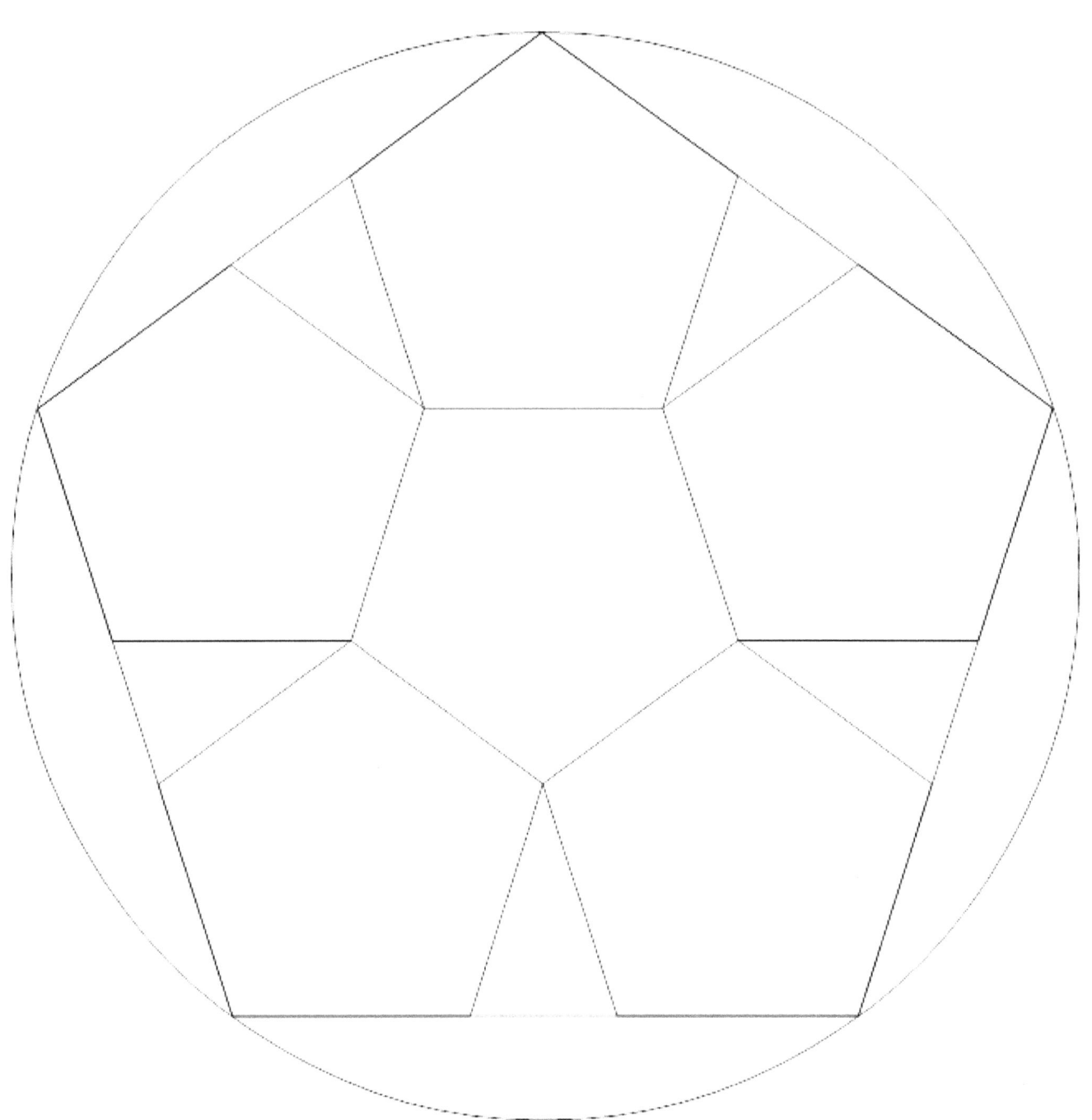

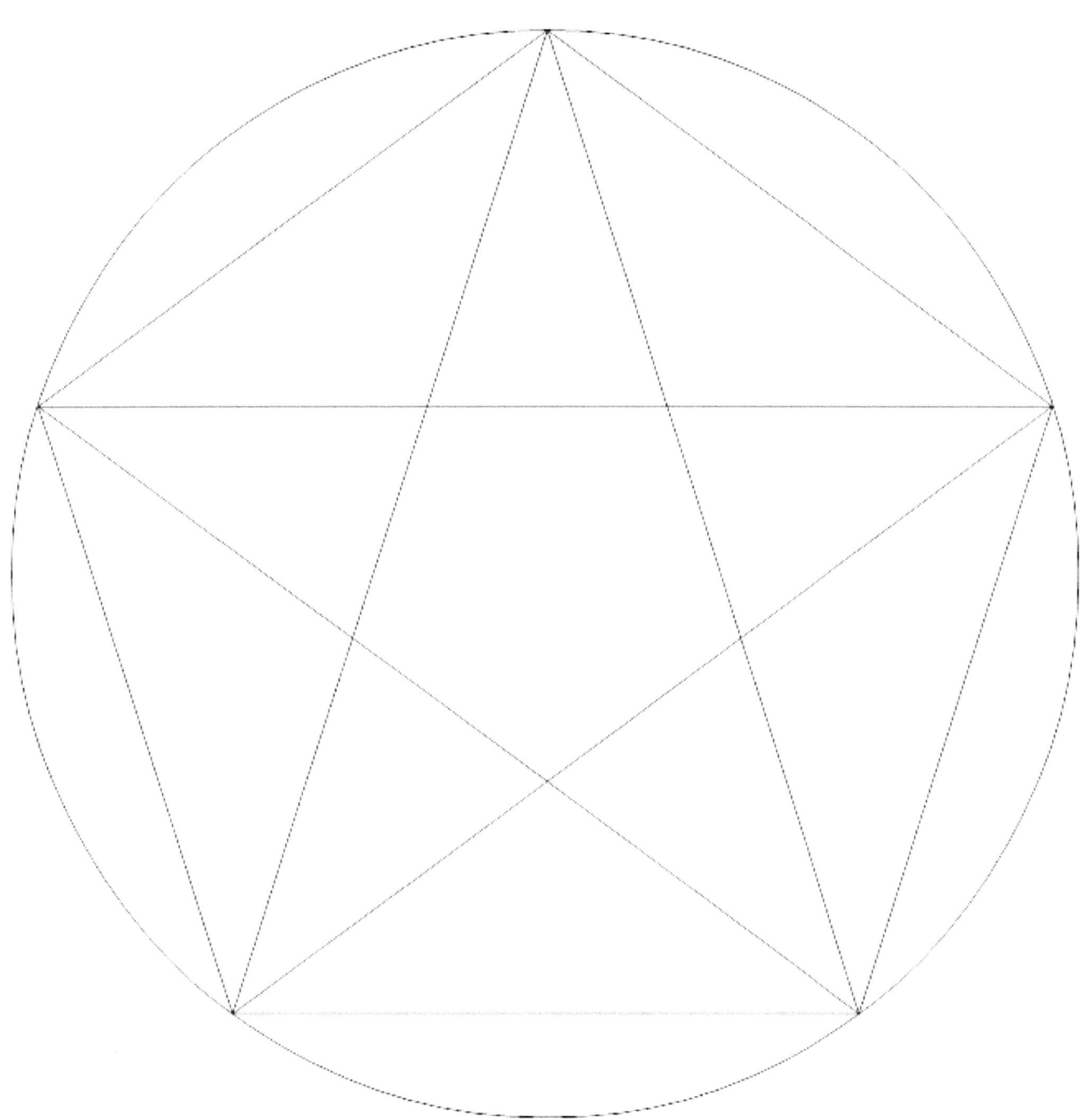

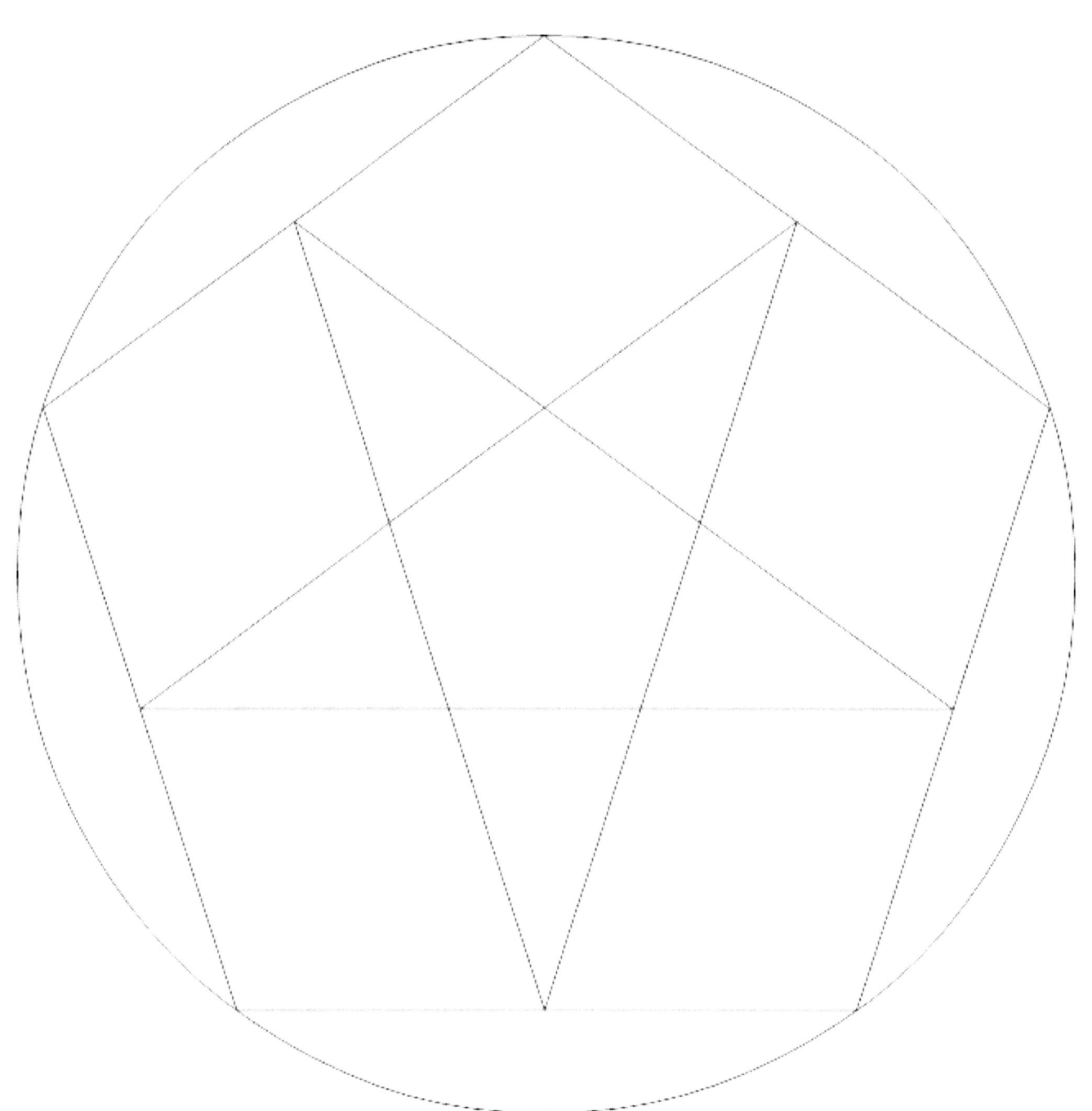

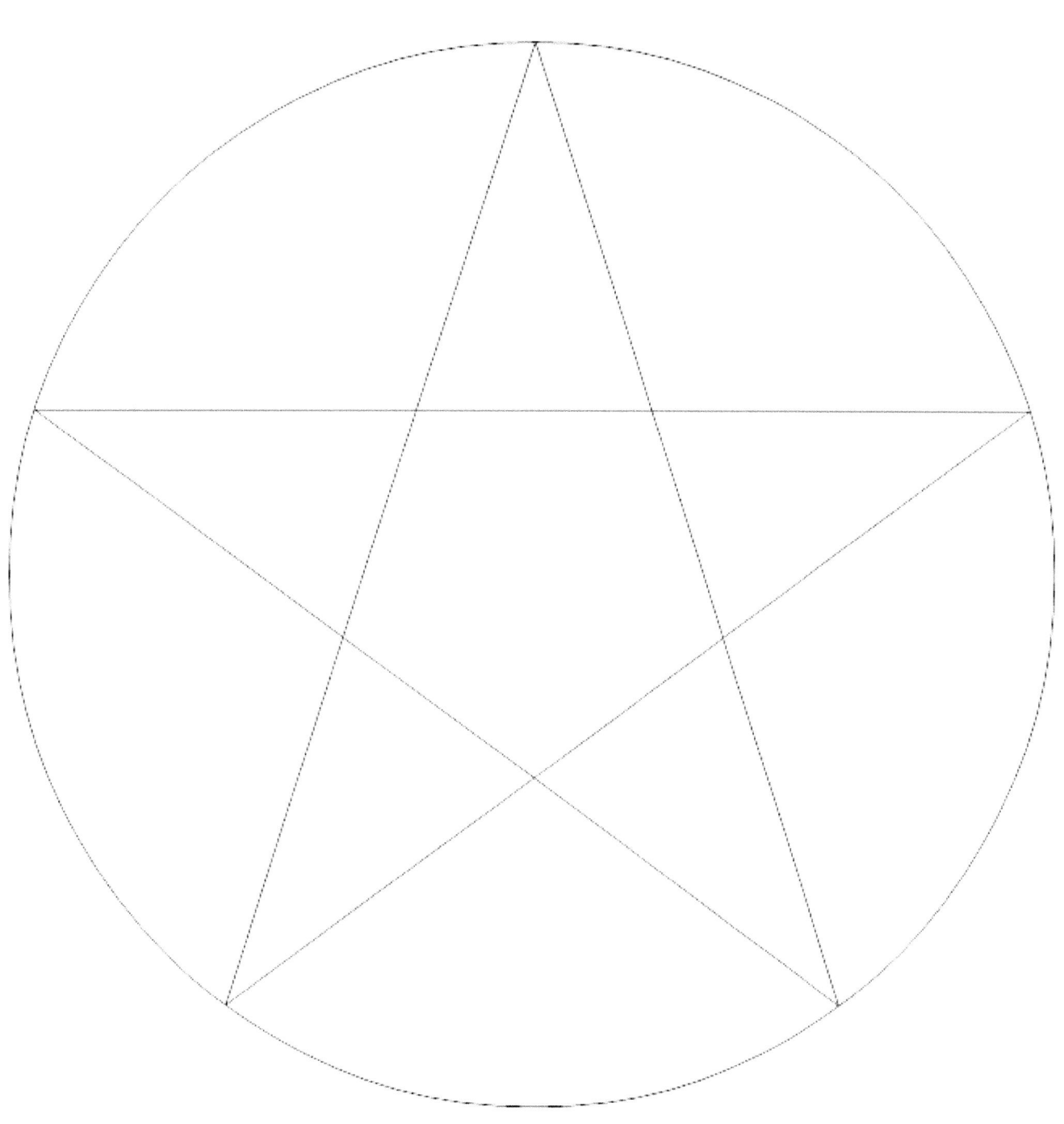

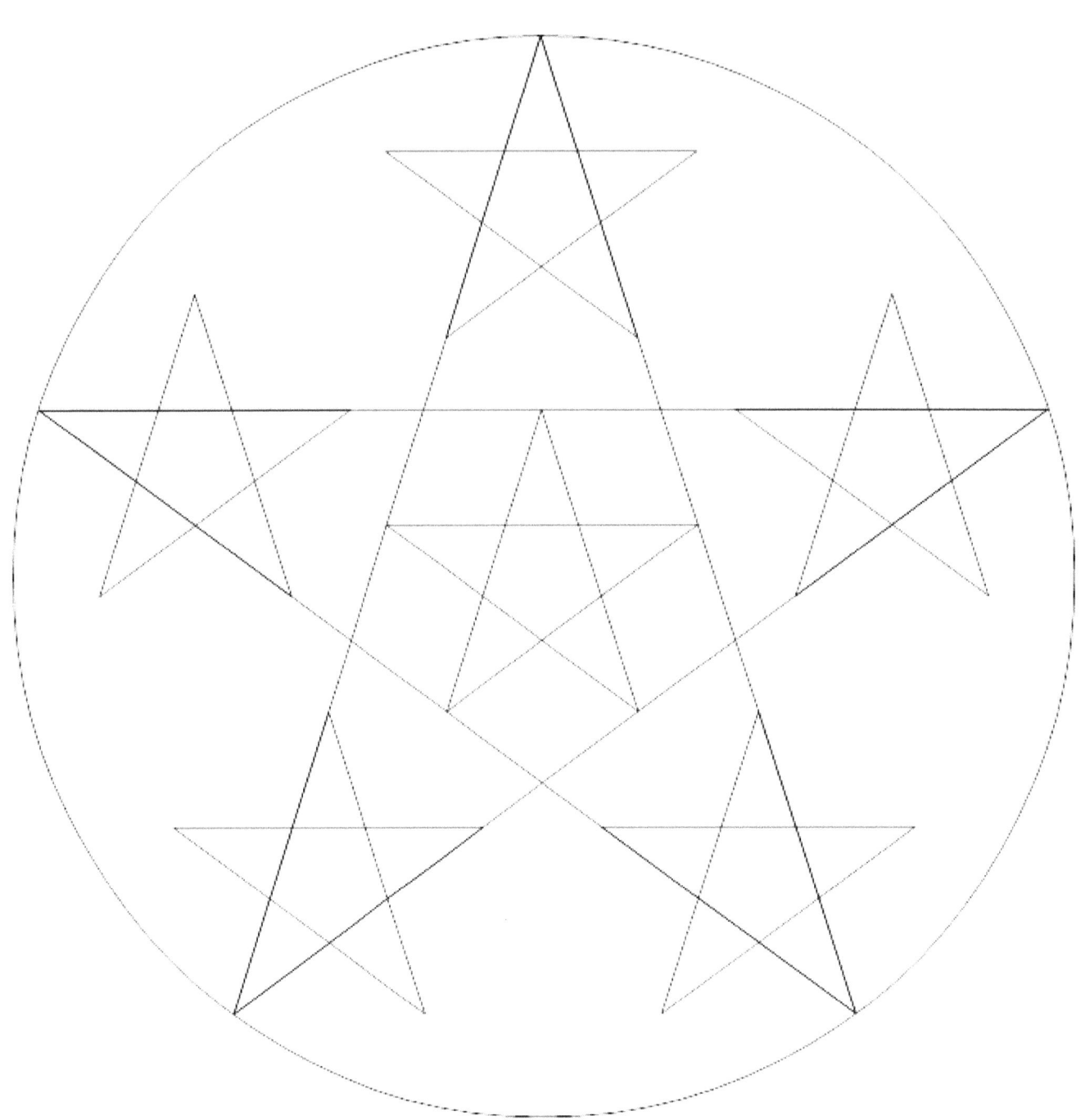

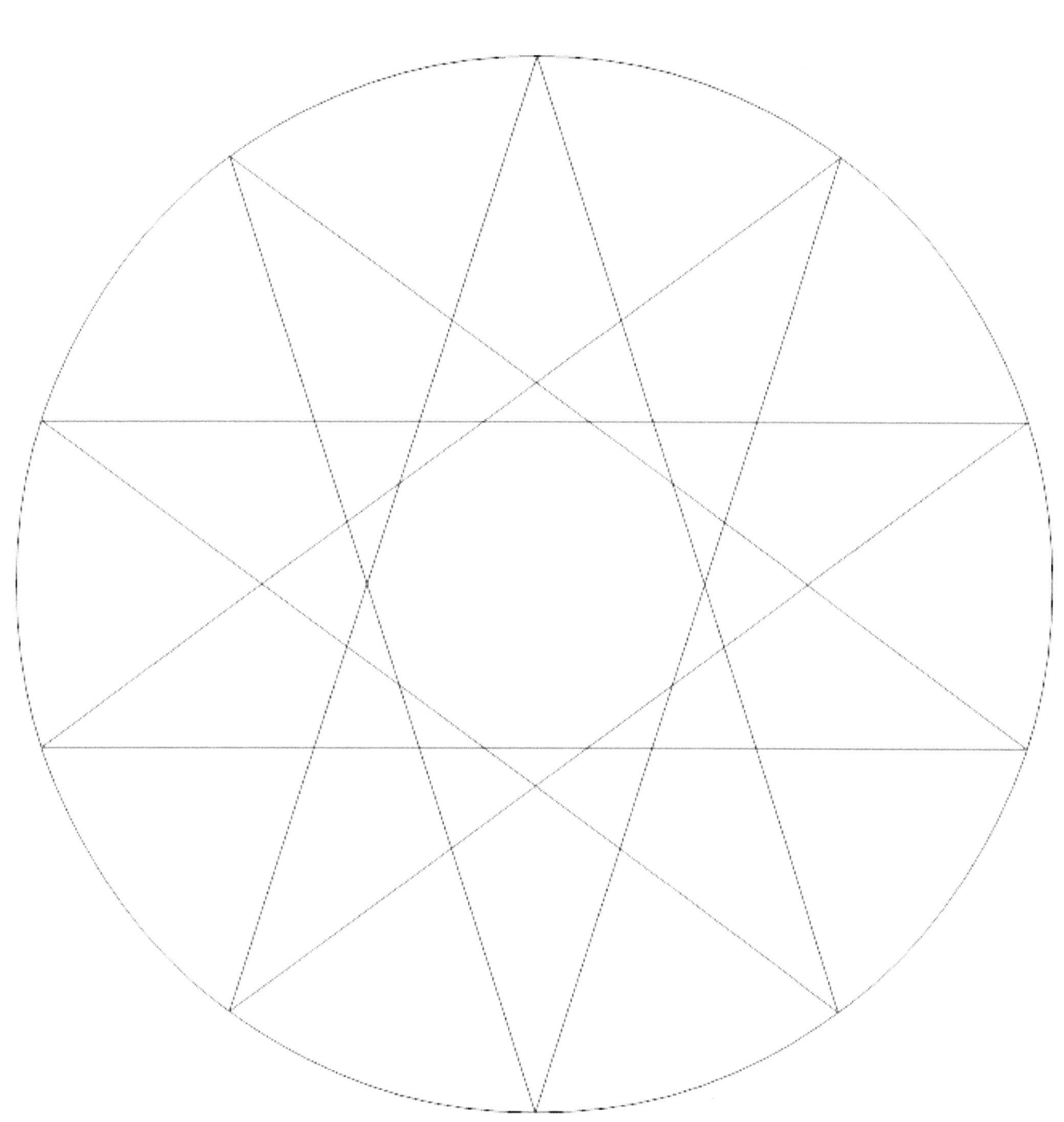

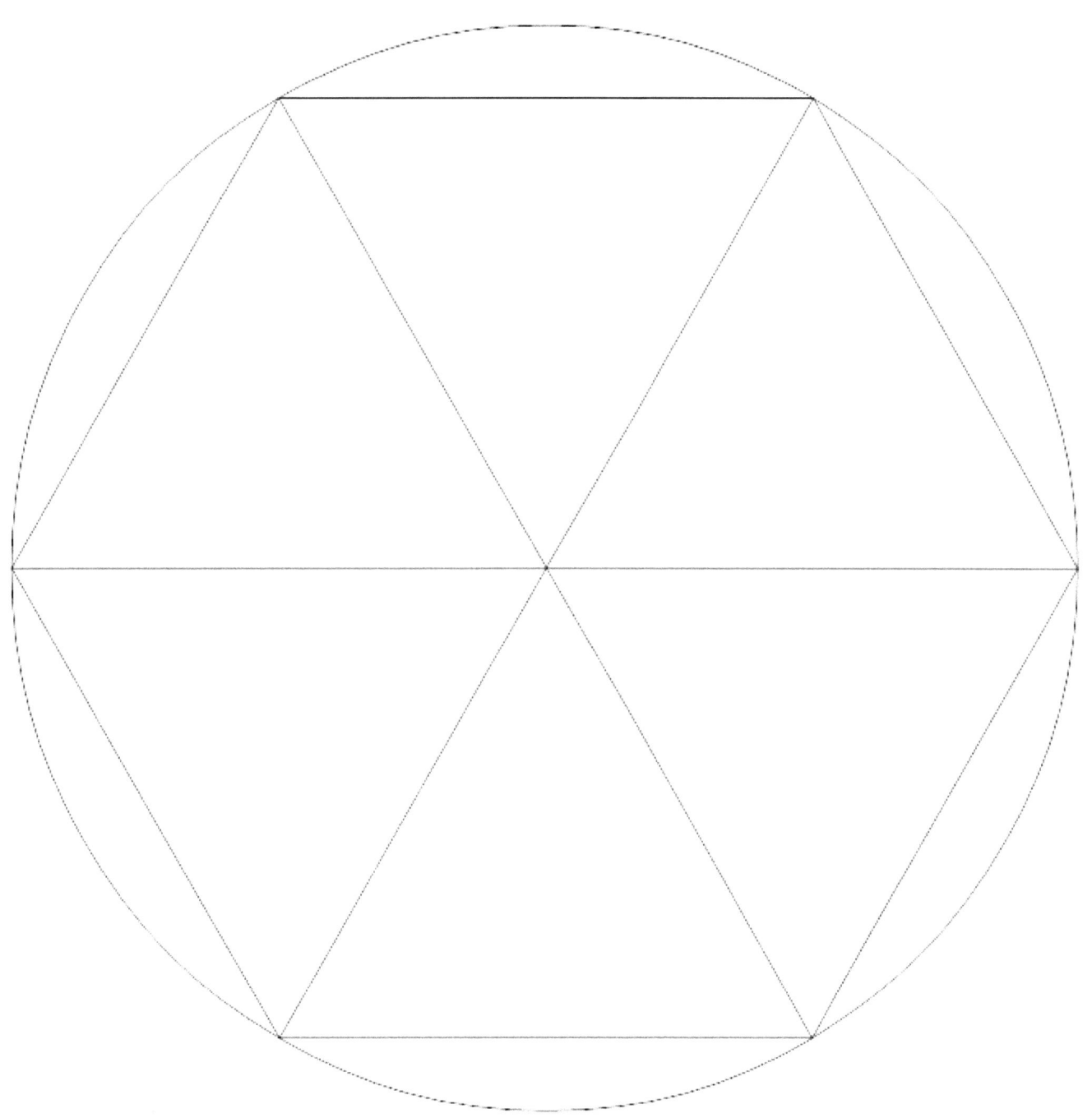

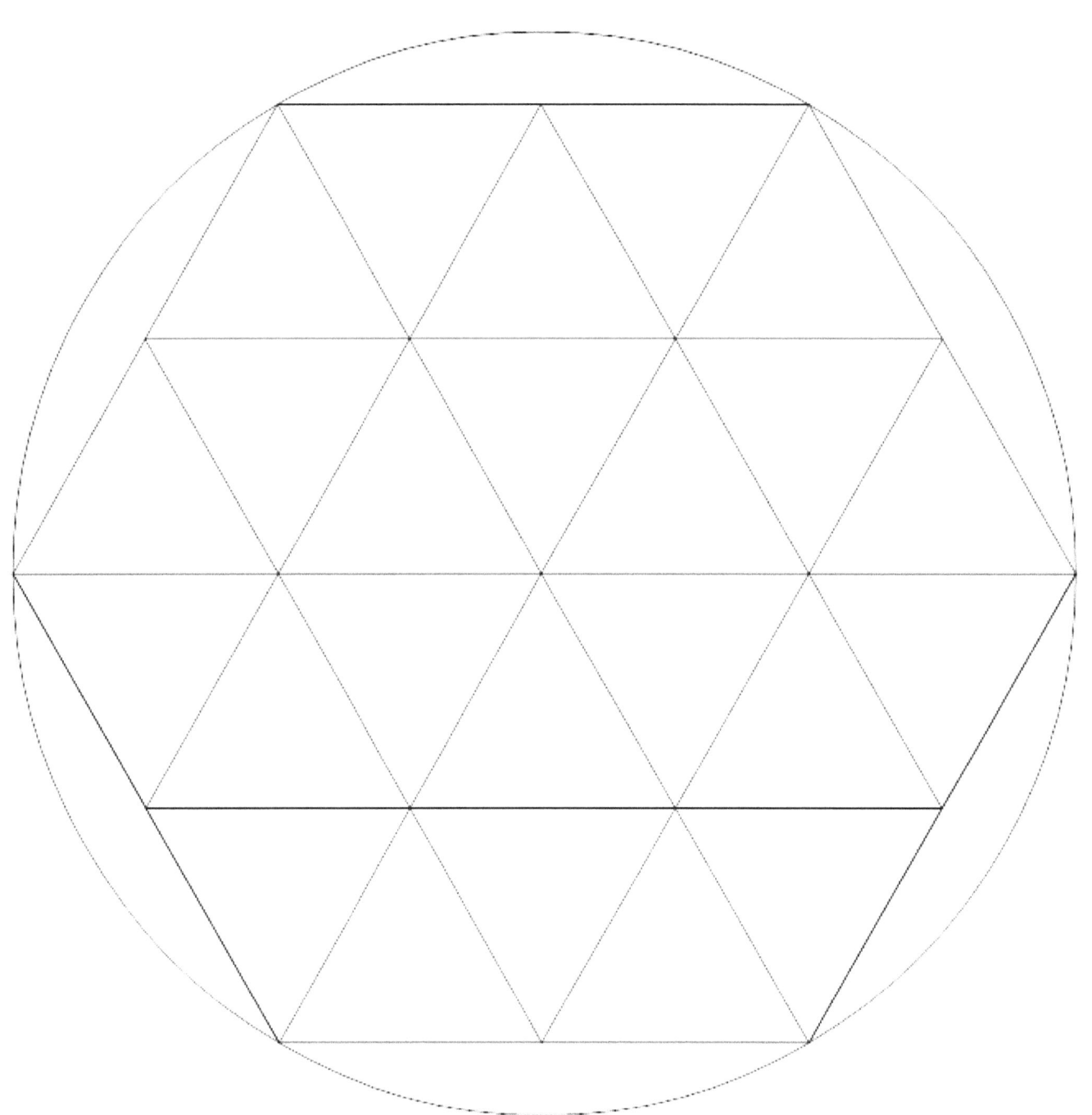

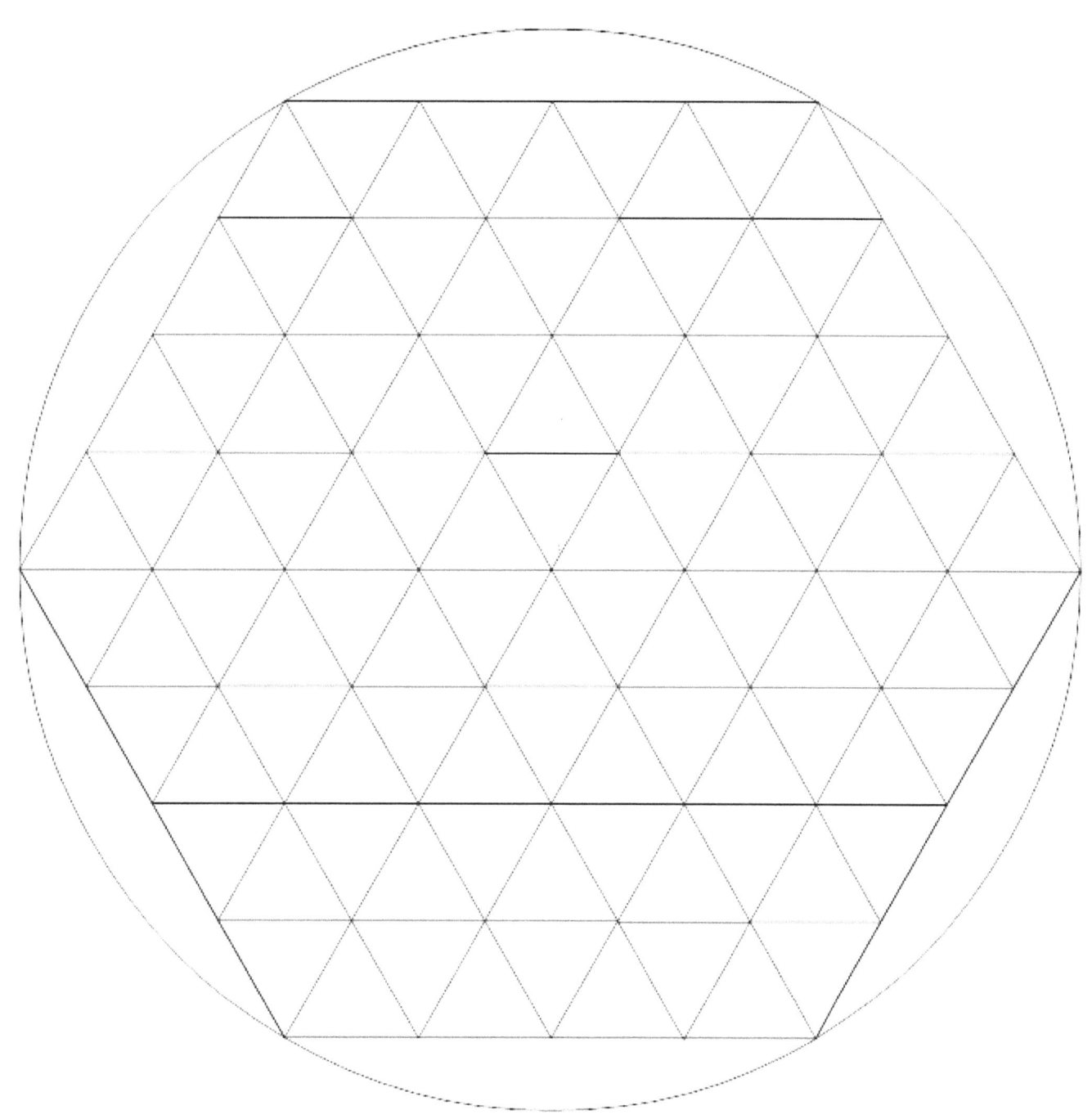

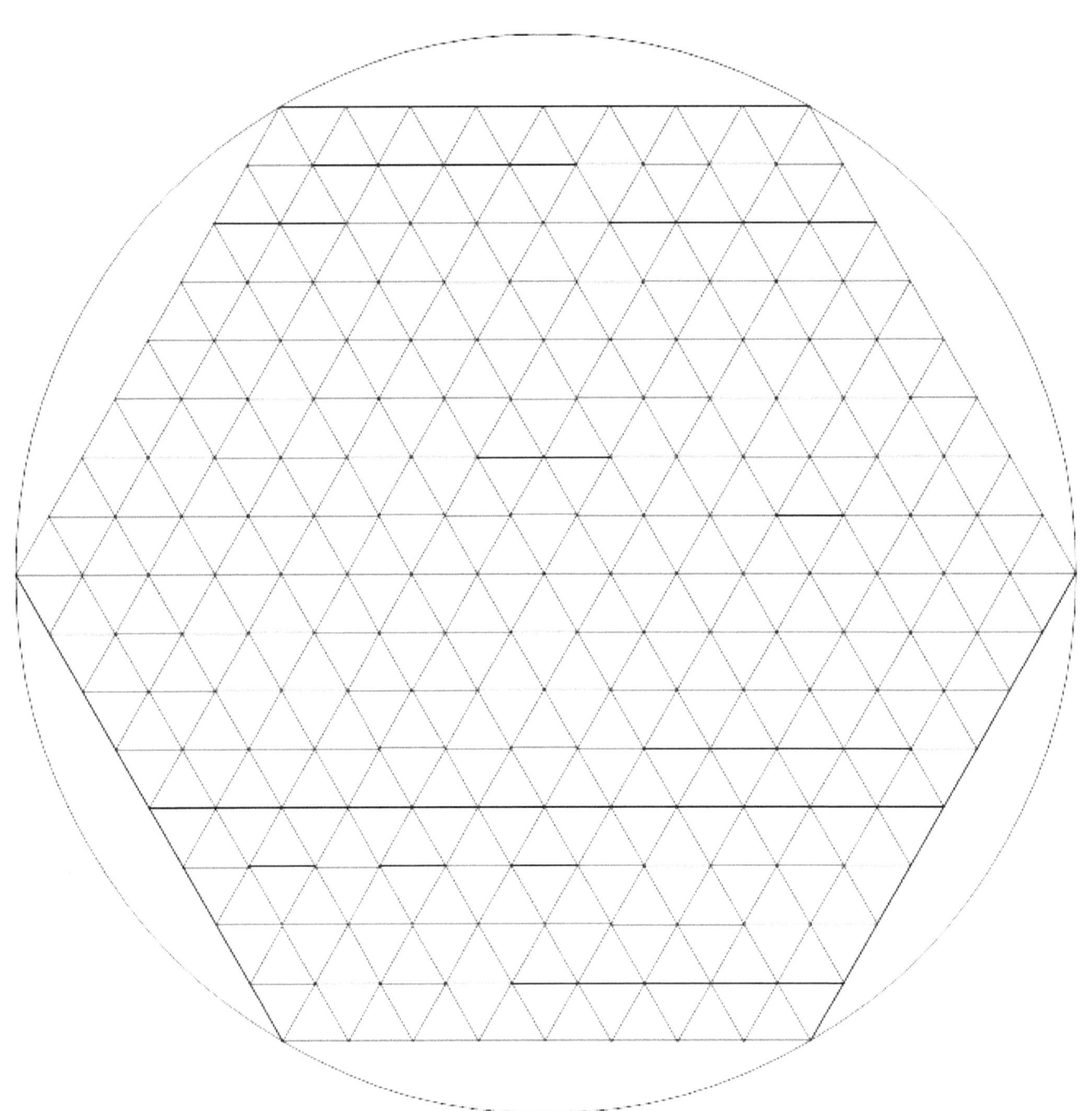

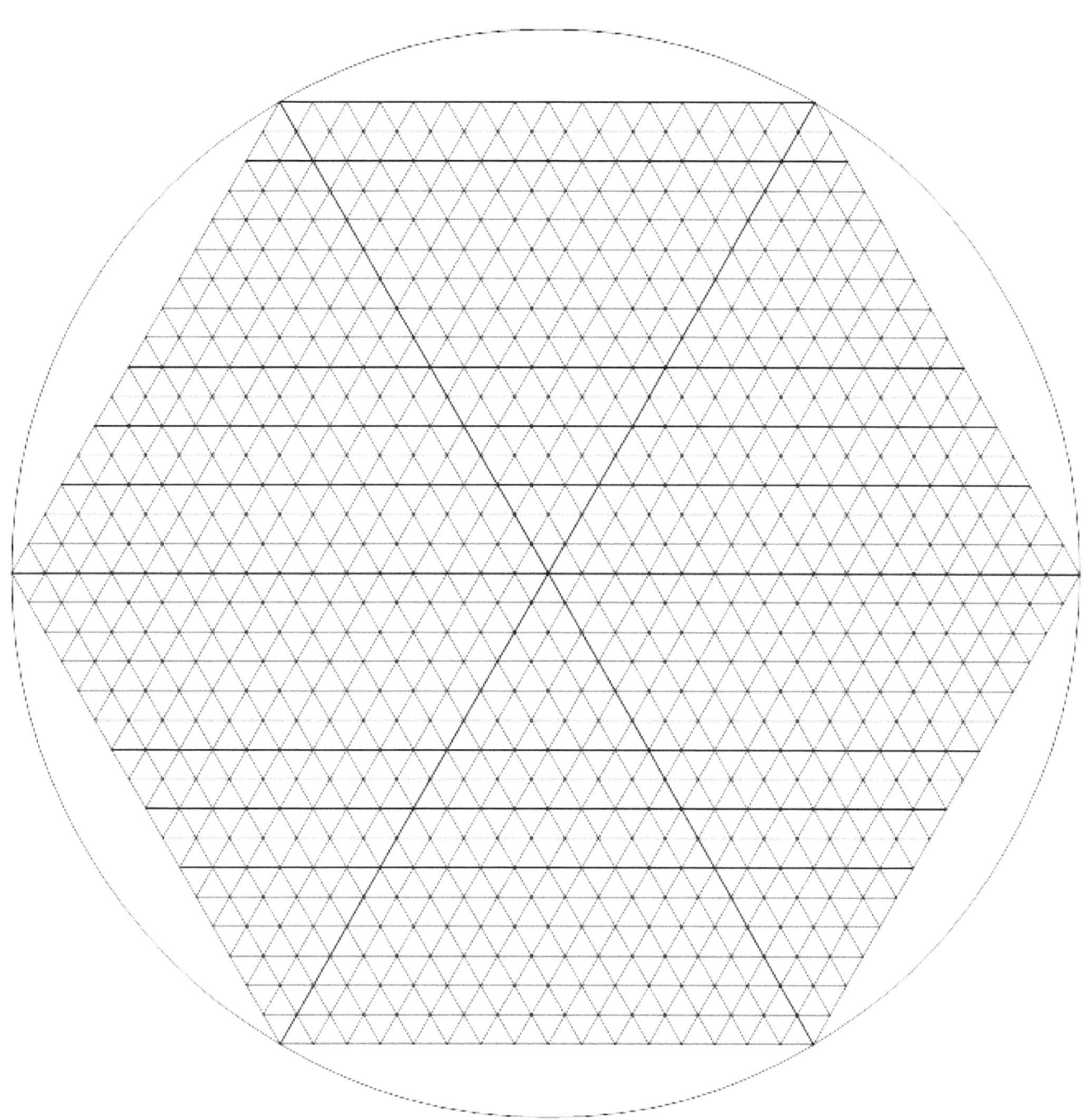

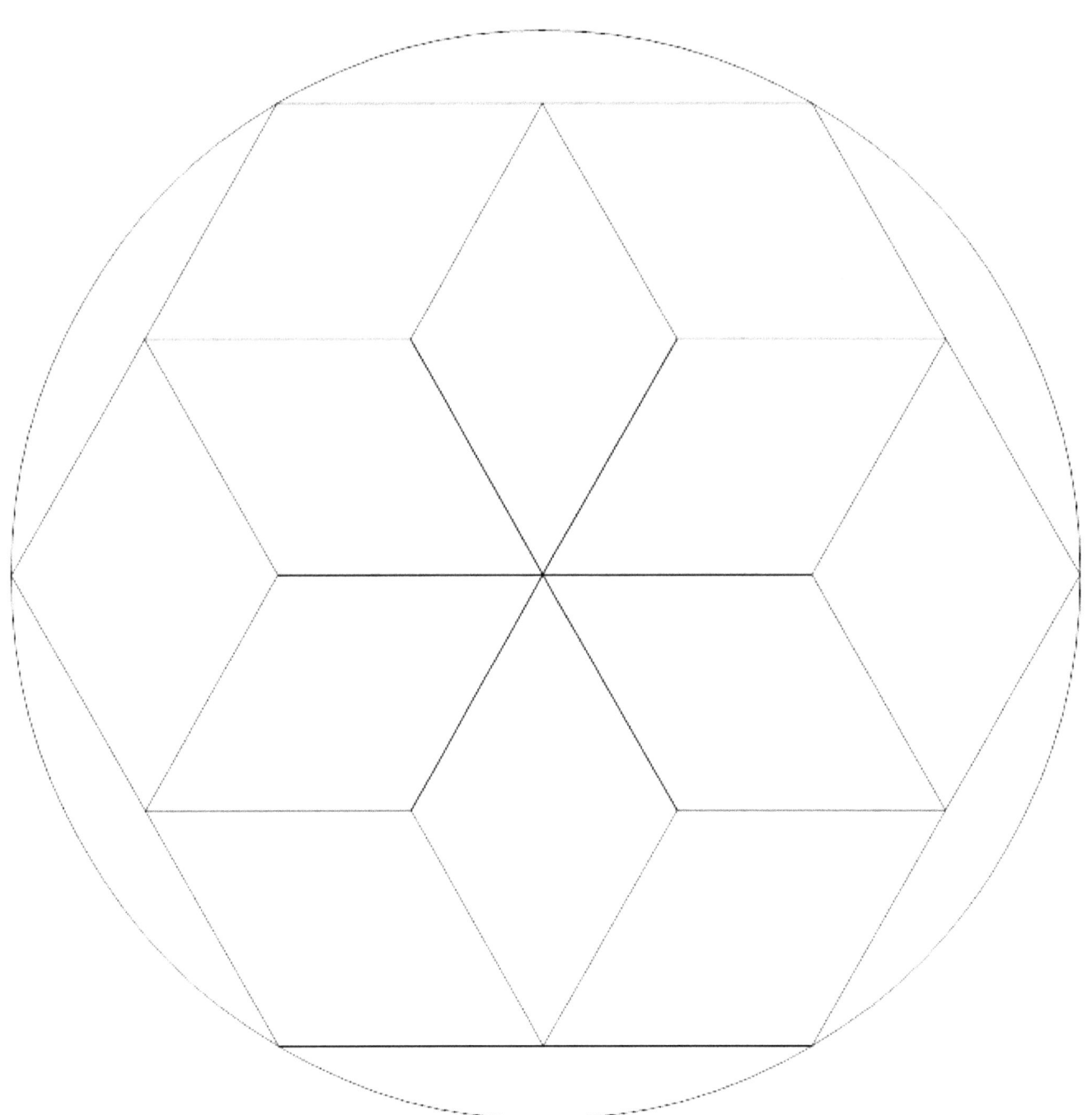

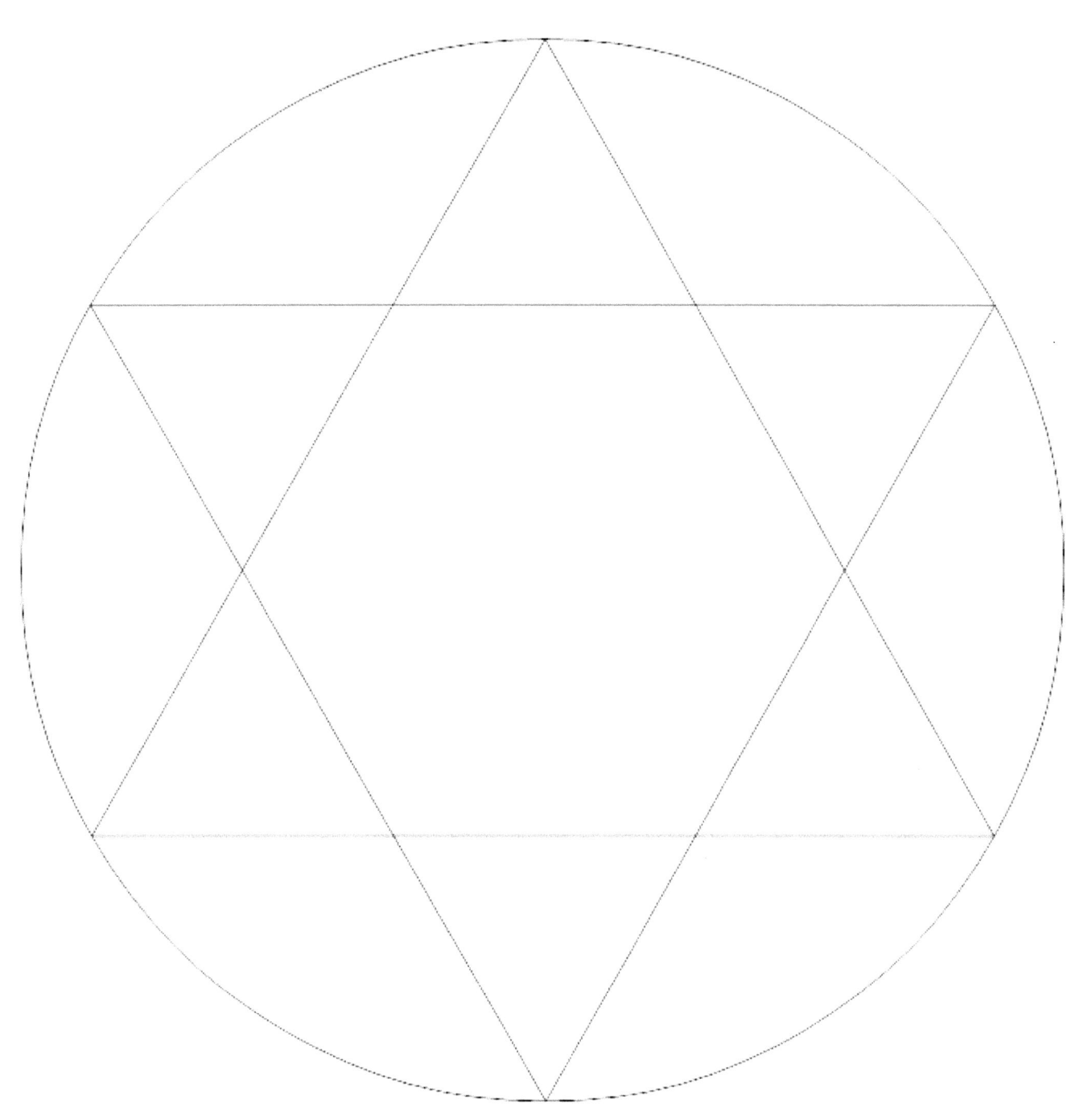

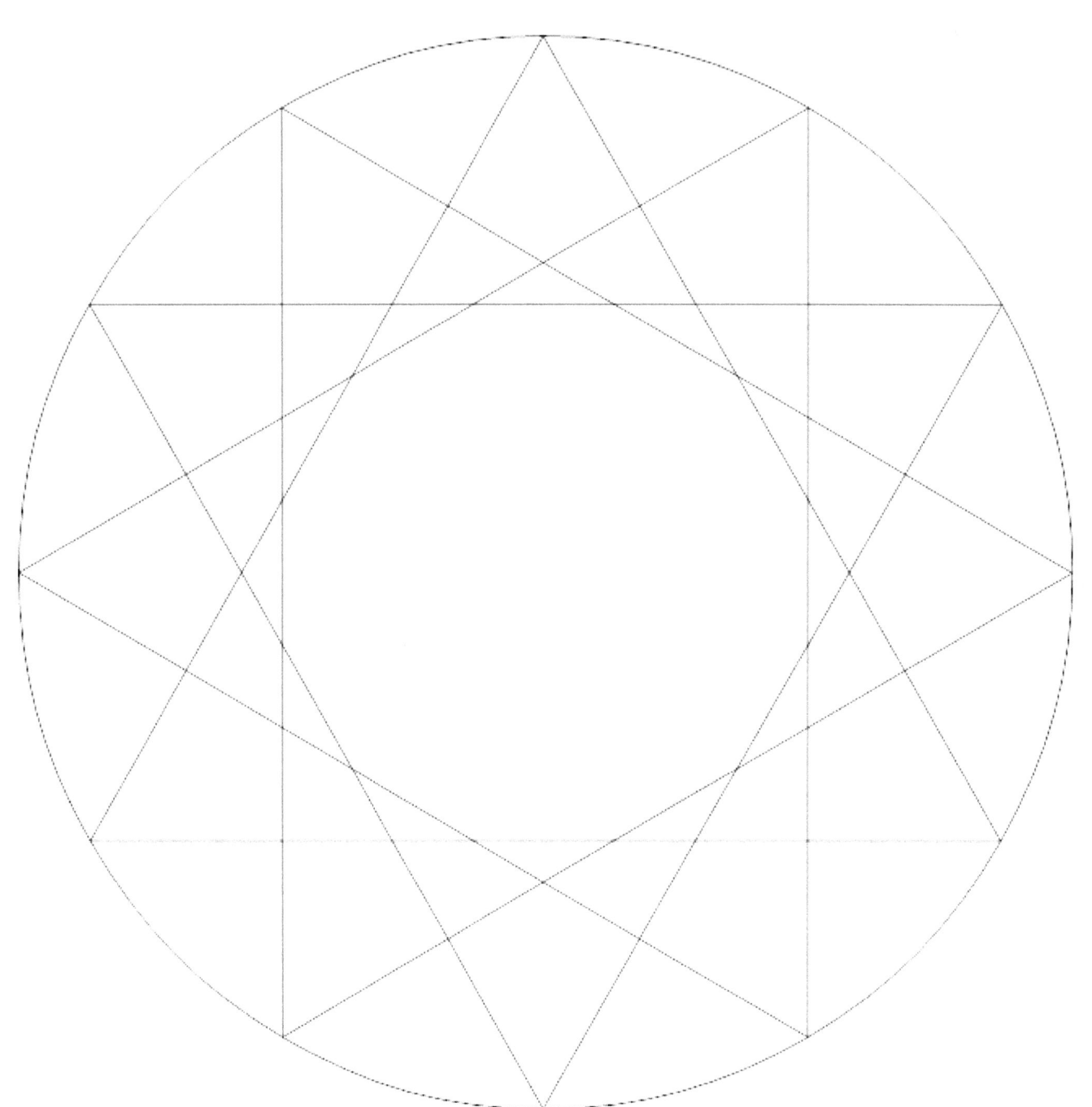

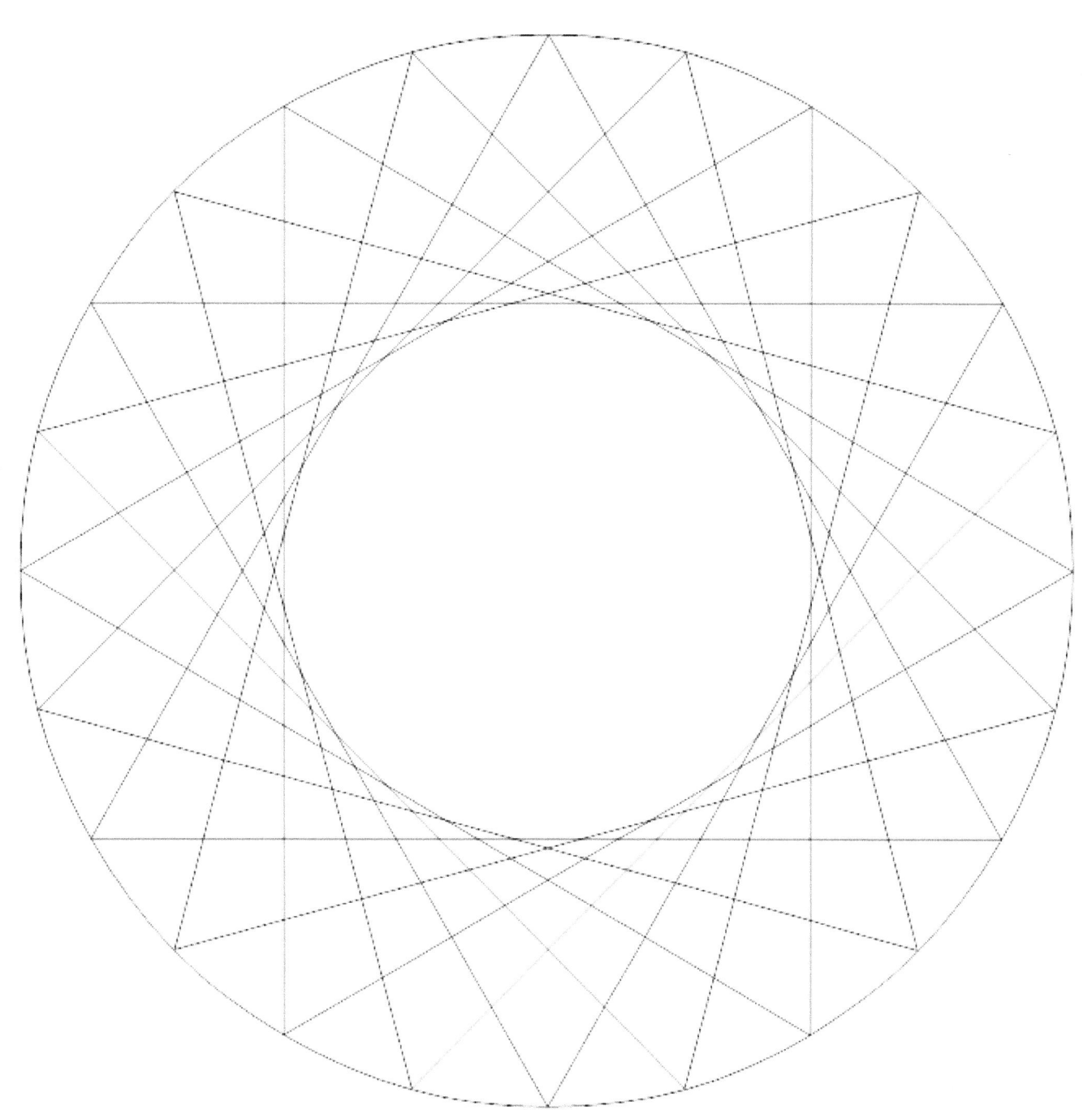

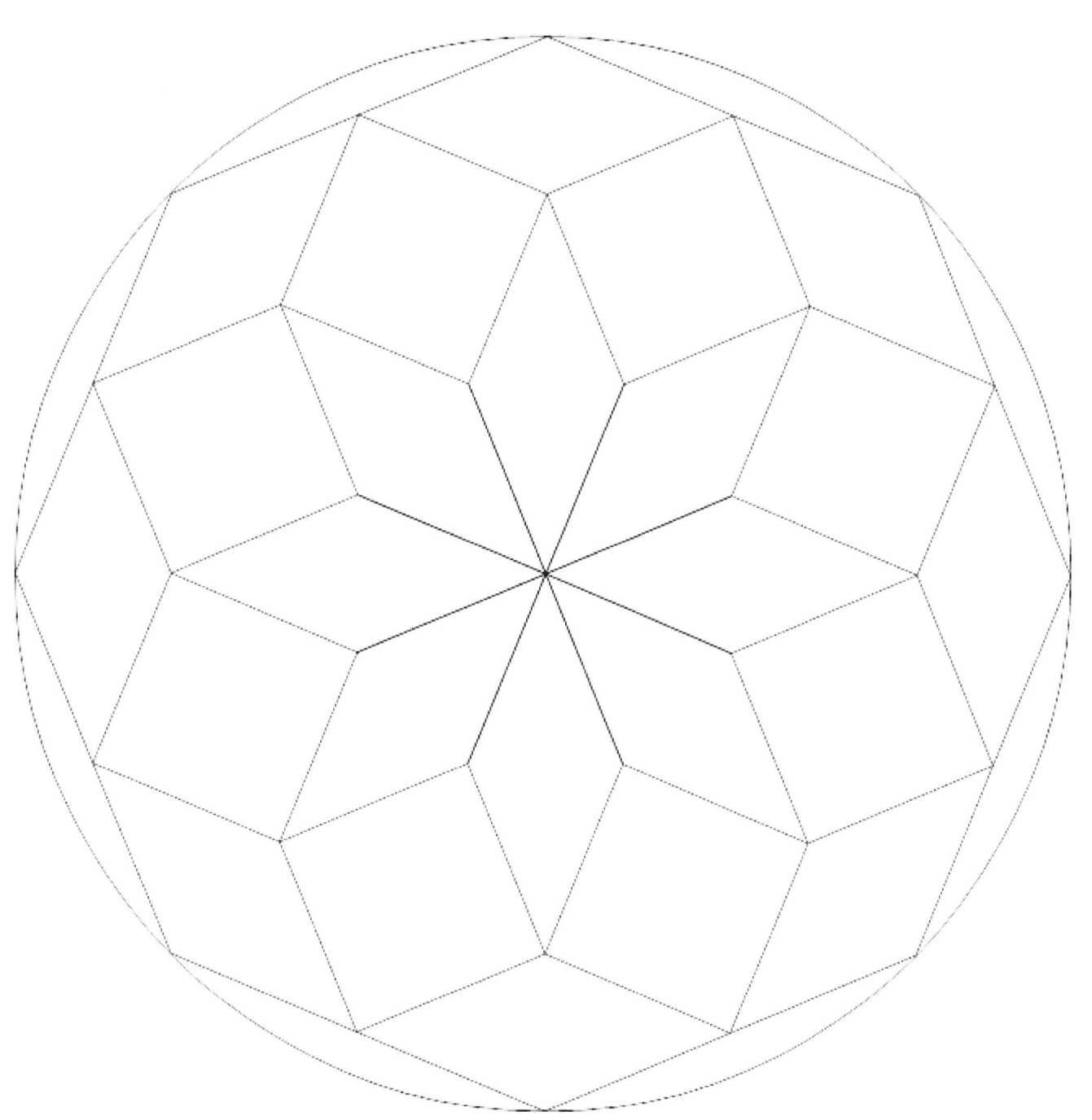

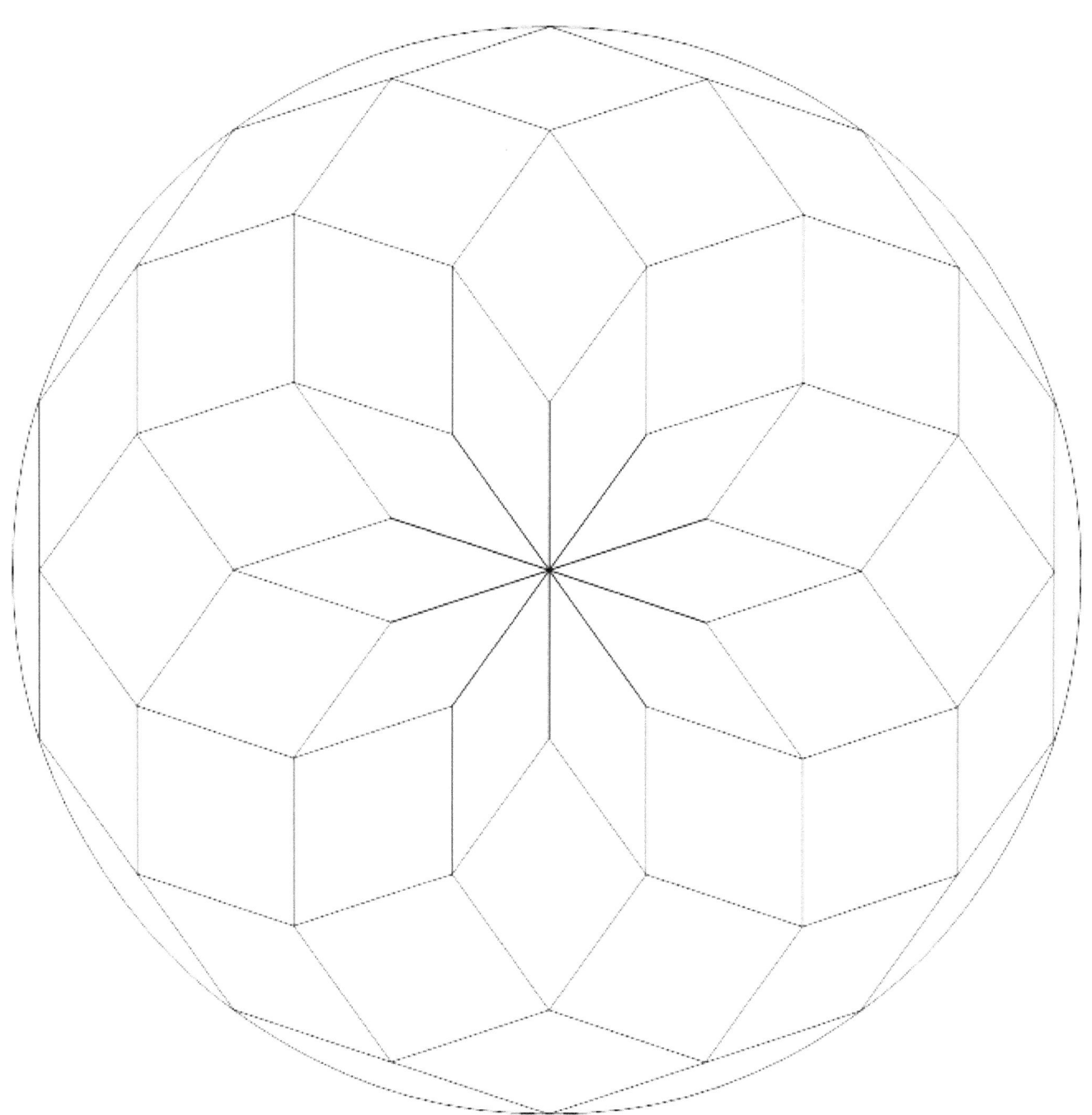

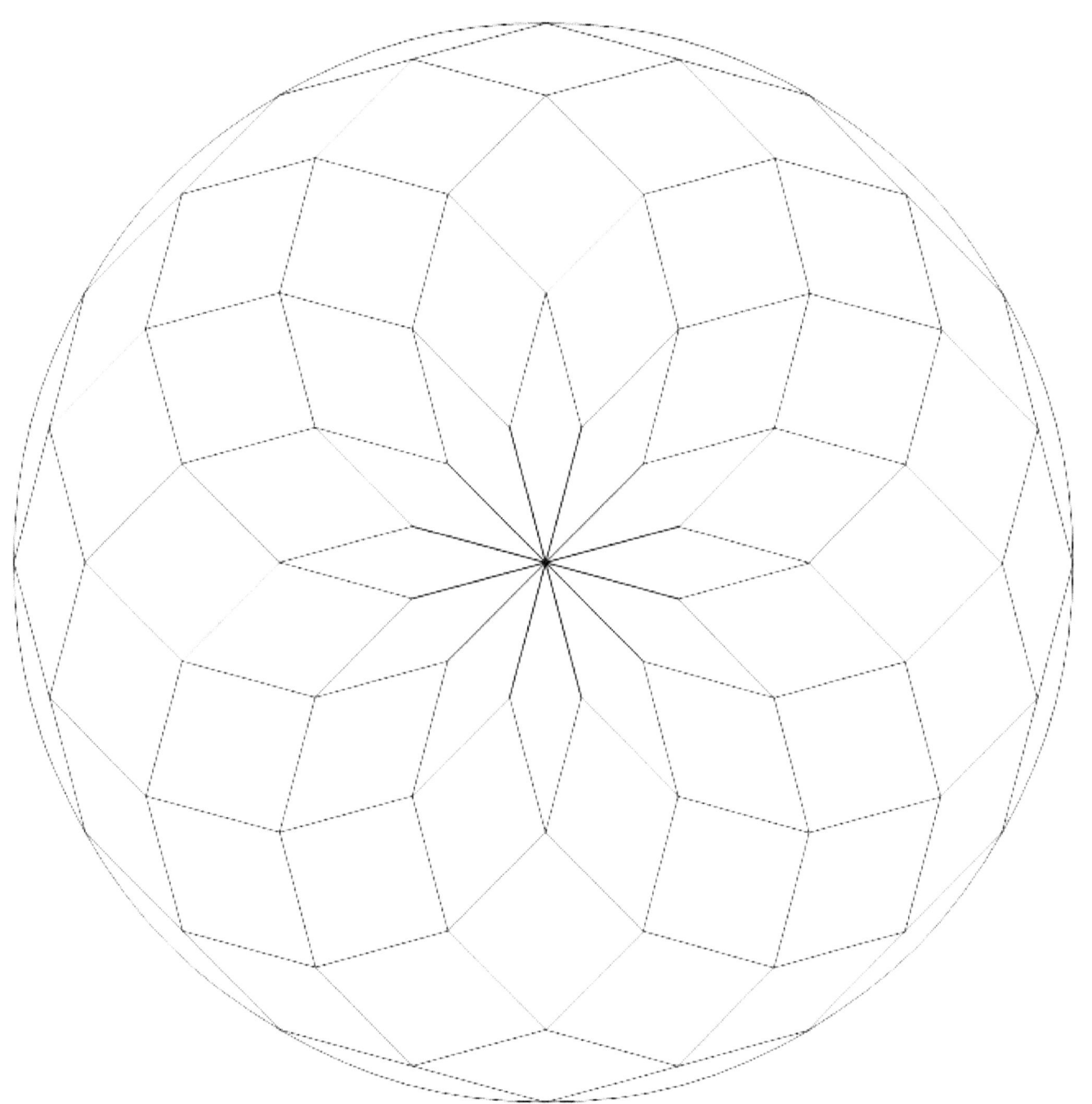

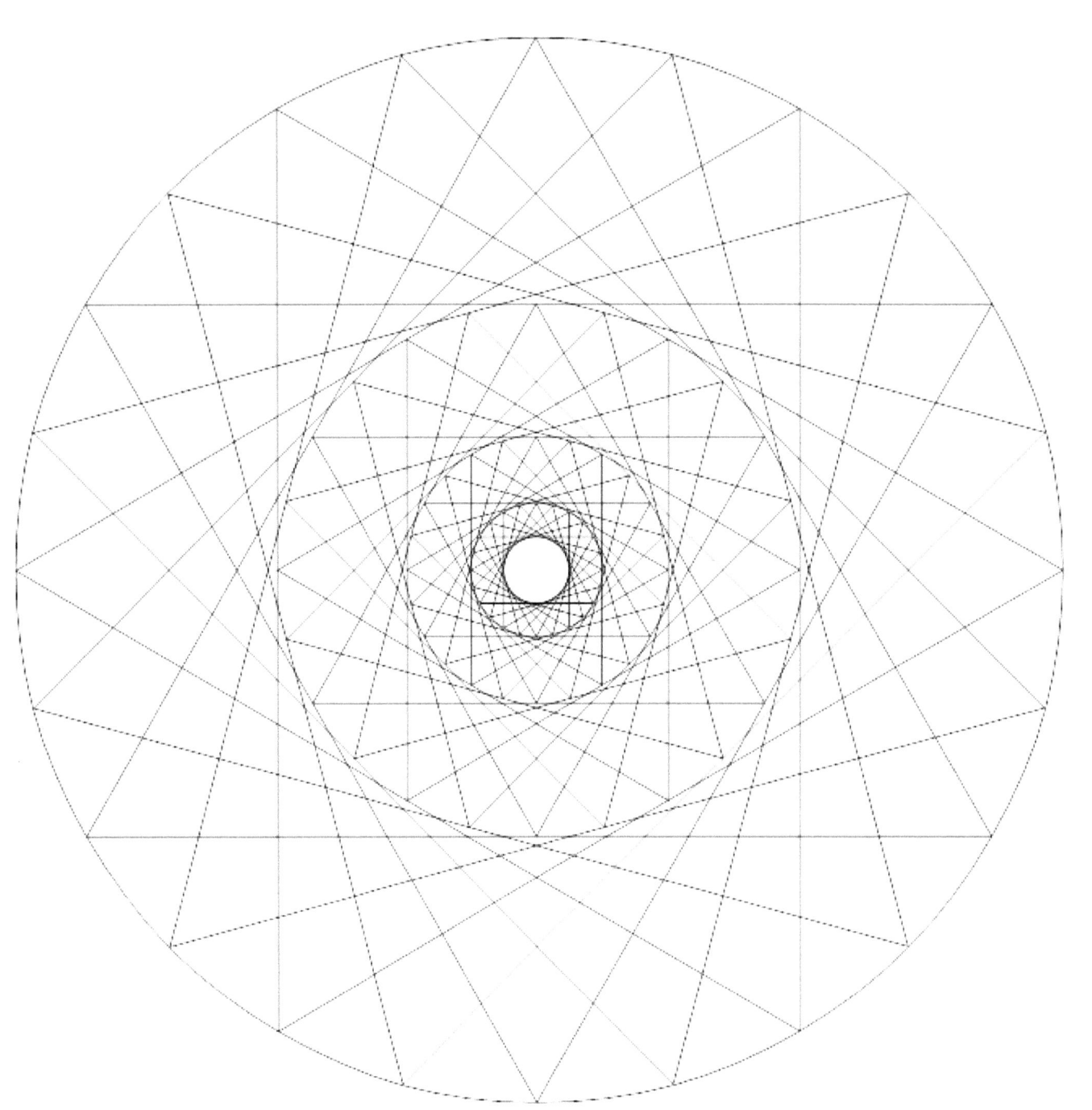

The Following pages contain my previous art with the colors removed. They will look vaguely familiar to those who have seen my previous art book I published. In fact some may be completel obvious such as the Happy Cat, Happy Pumpkin, or Butterfly, but they will not look as cool until you color them yourself!

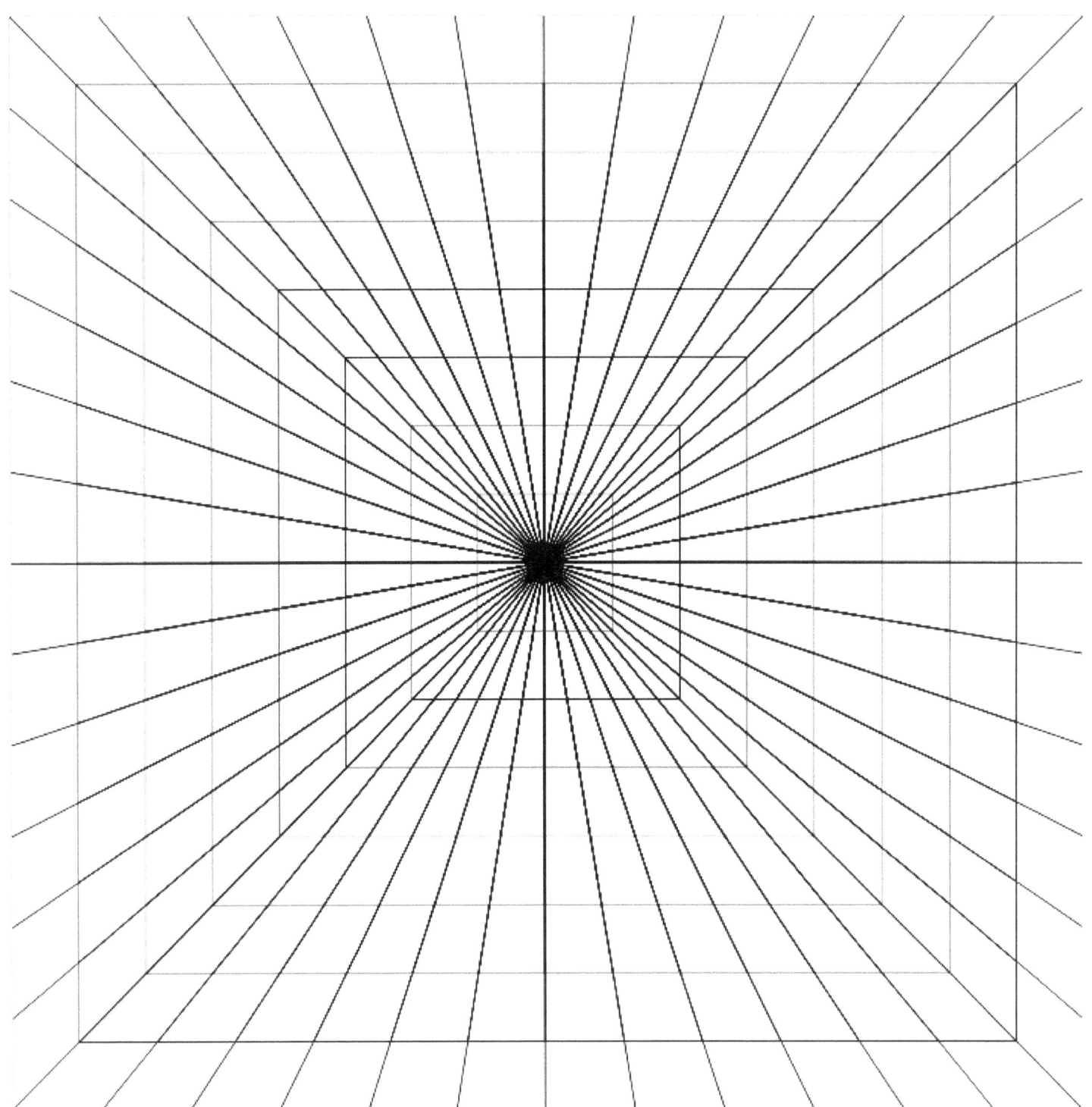

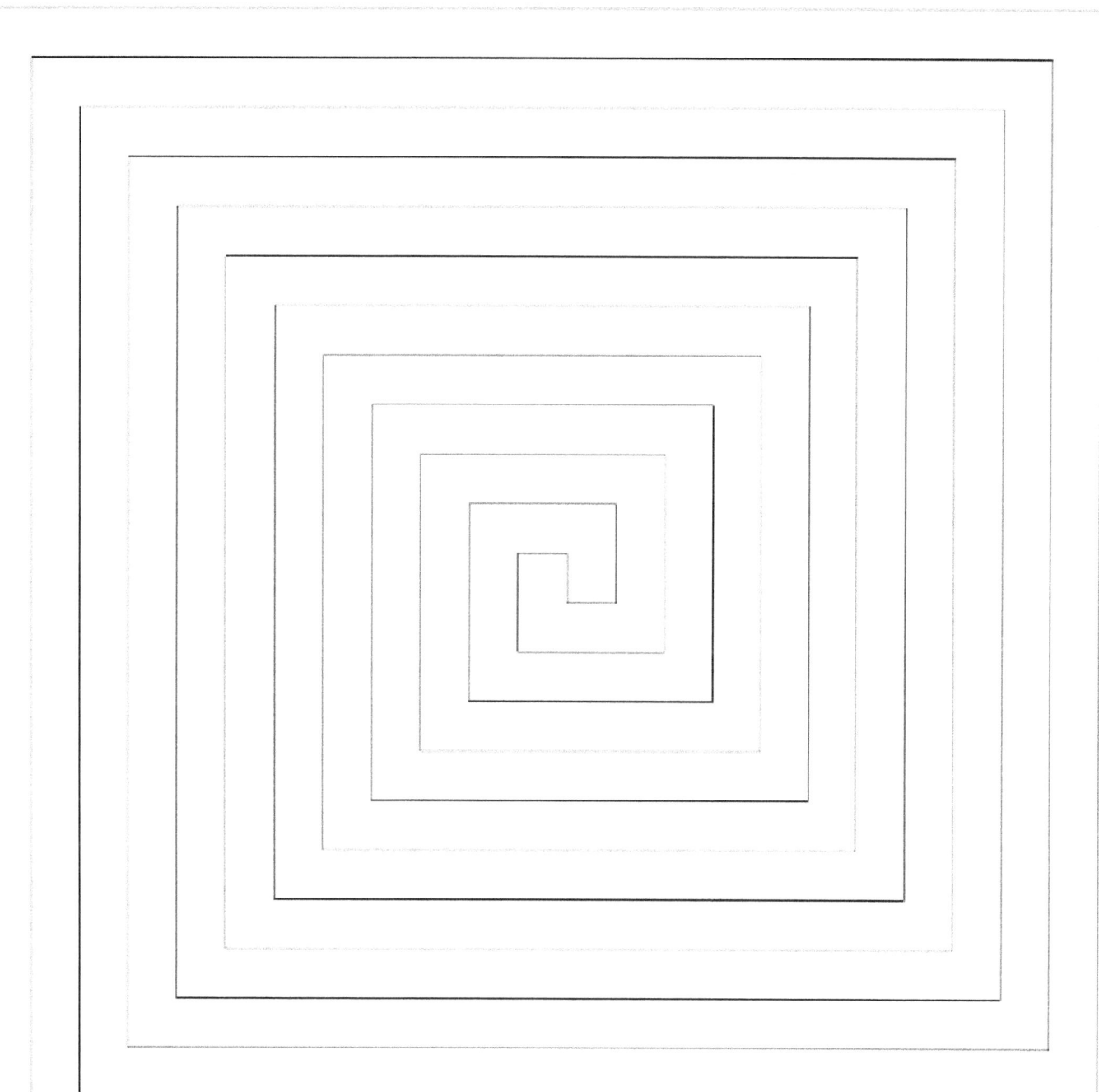

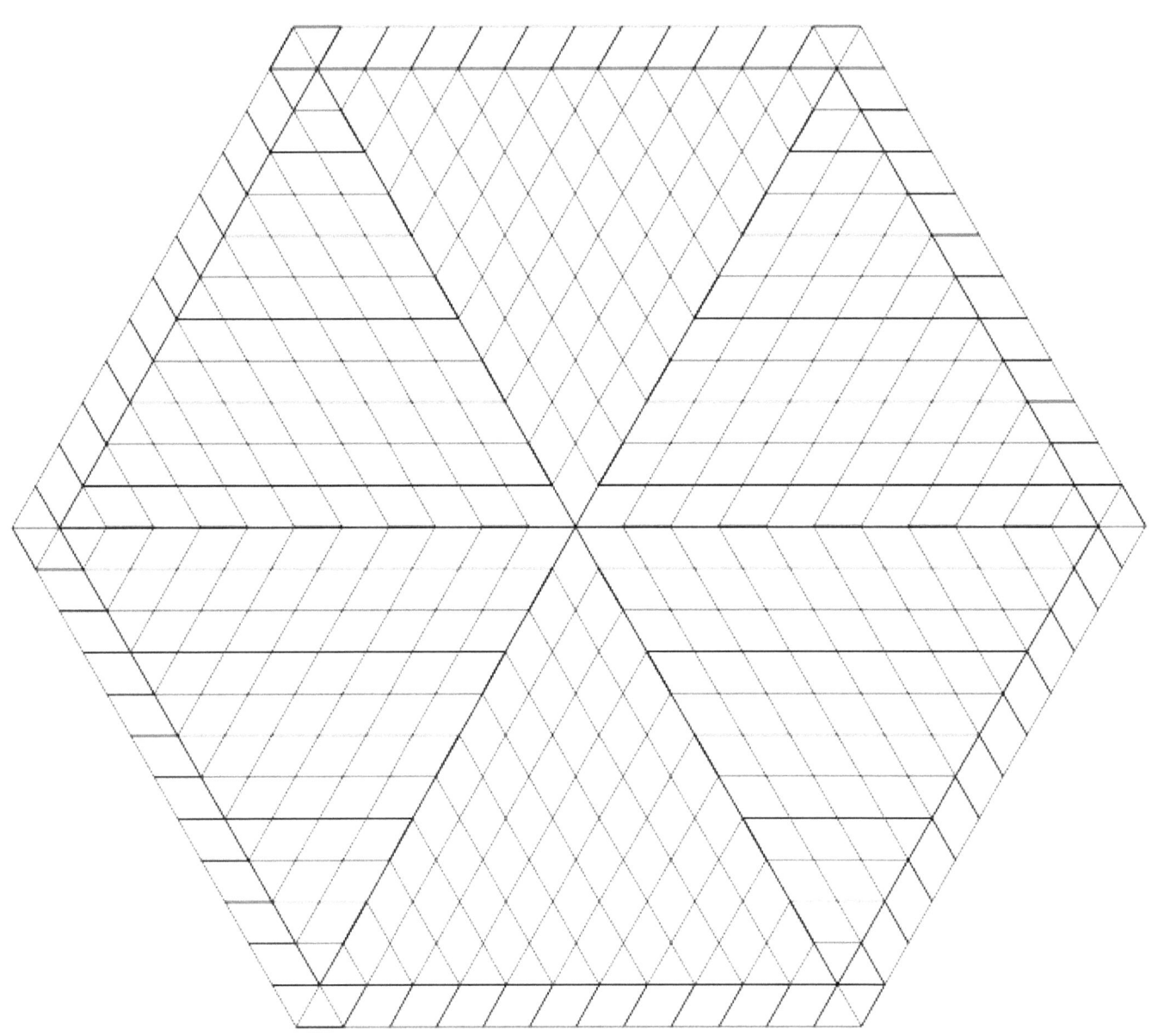

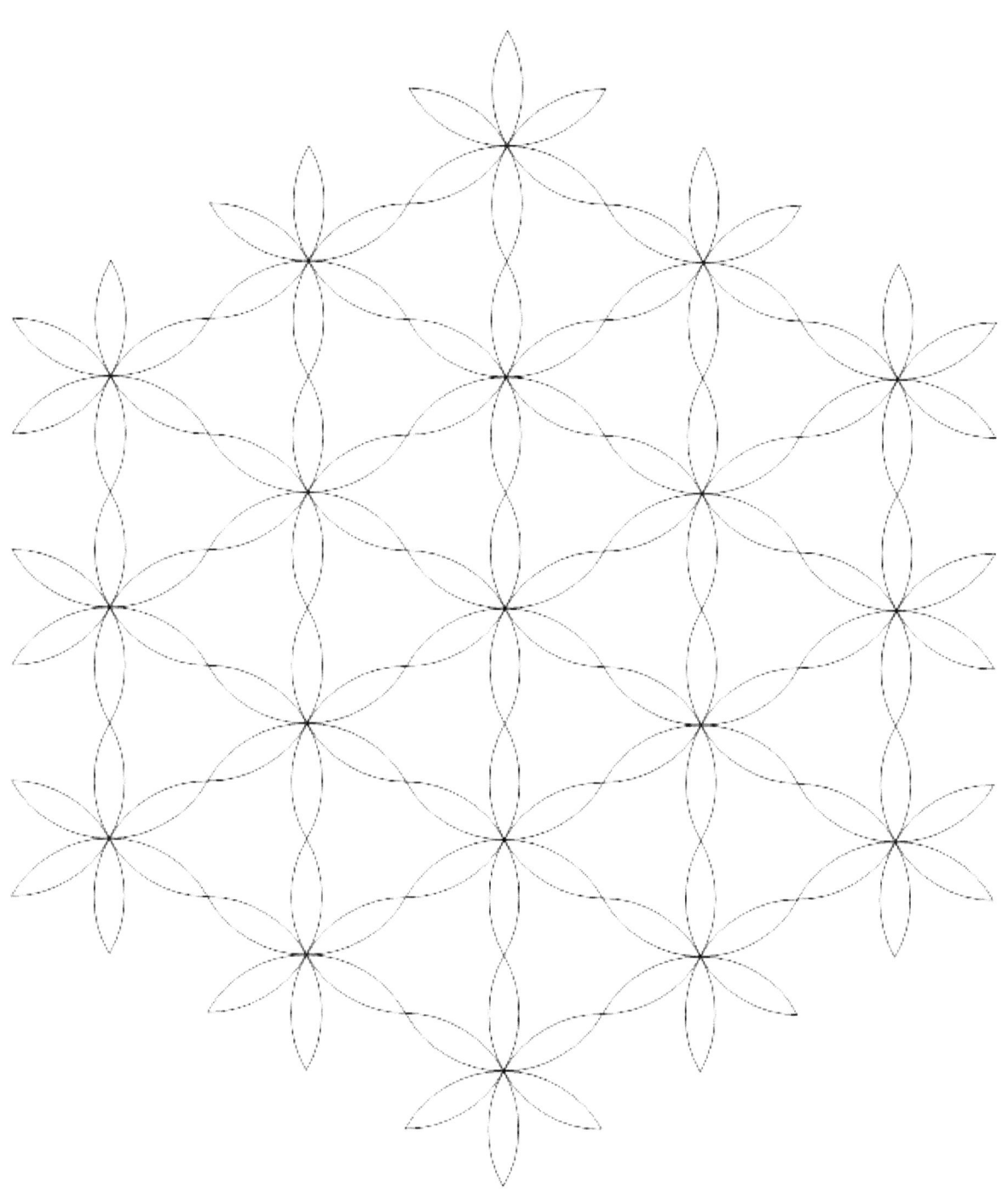

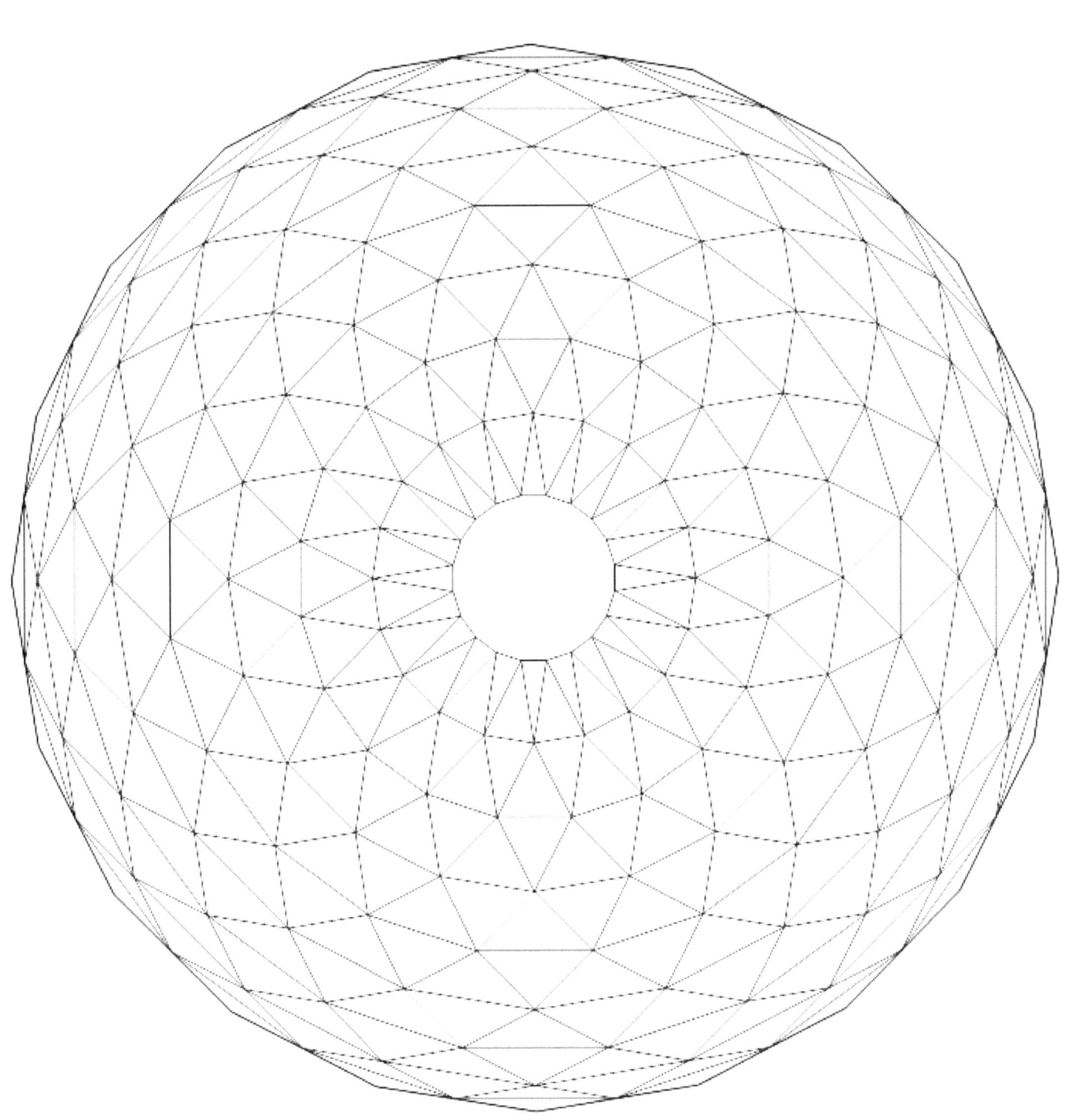

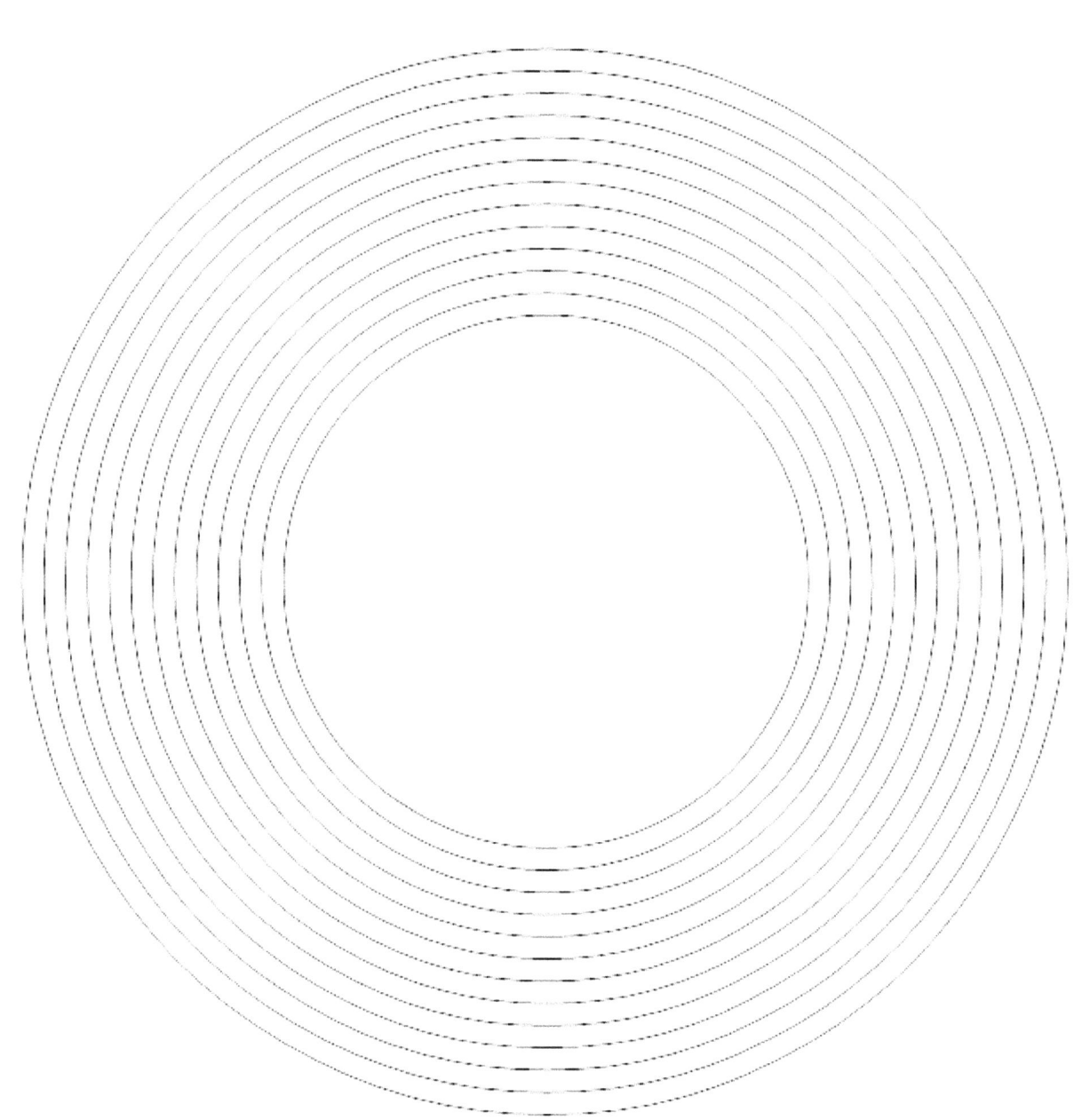

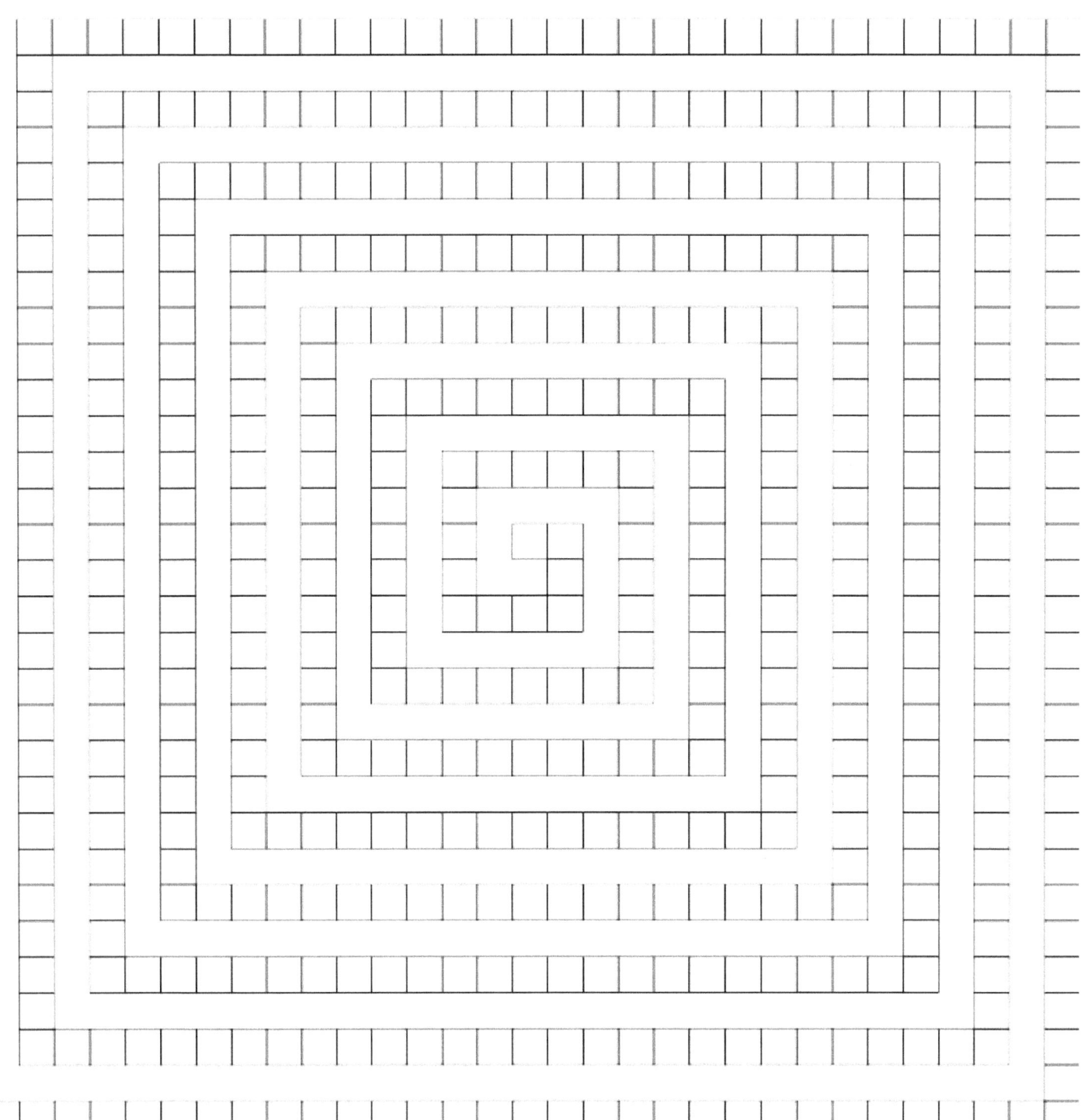

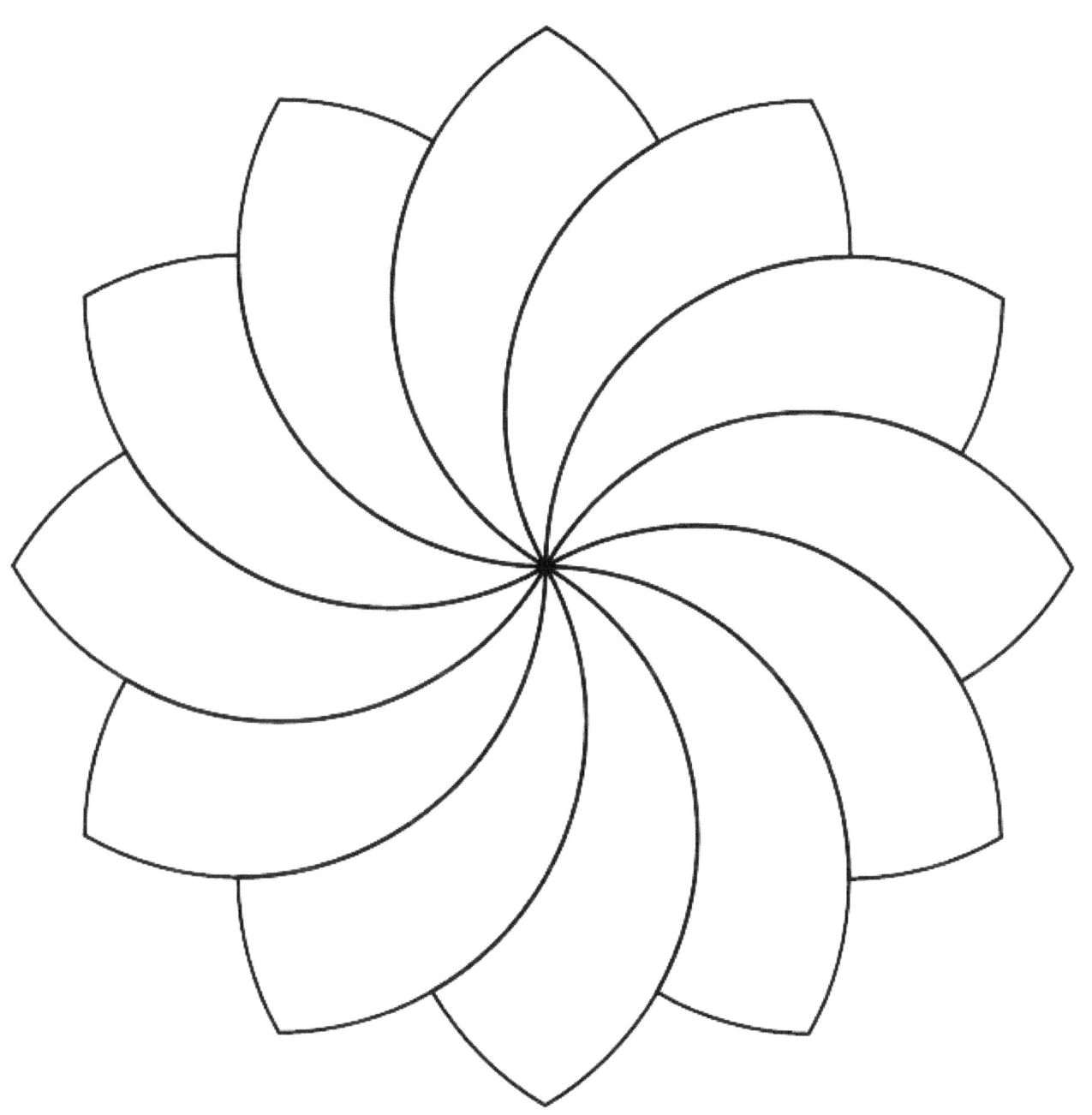

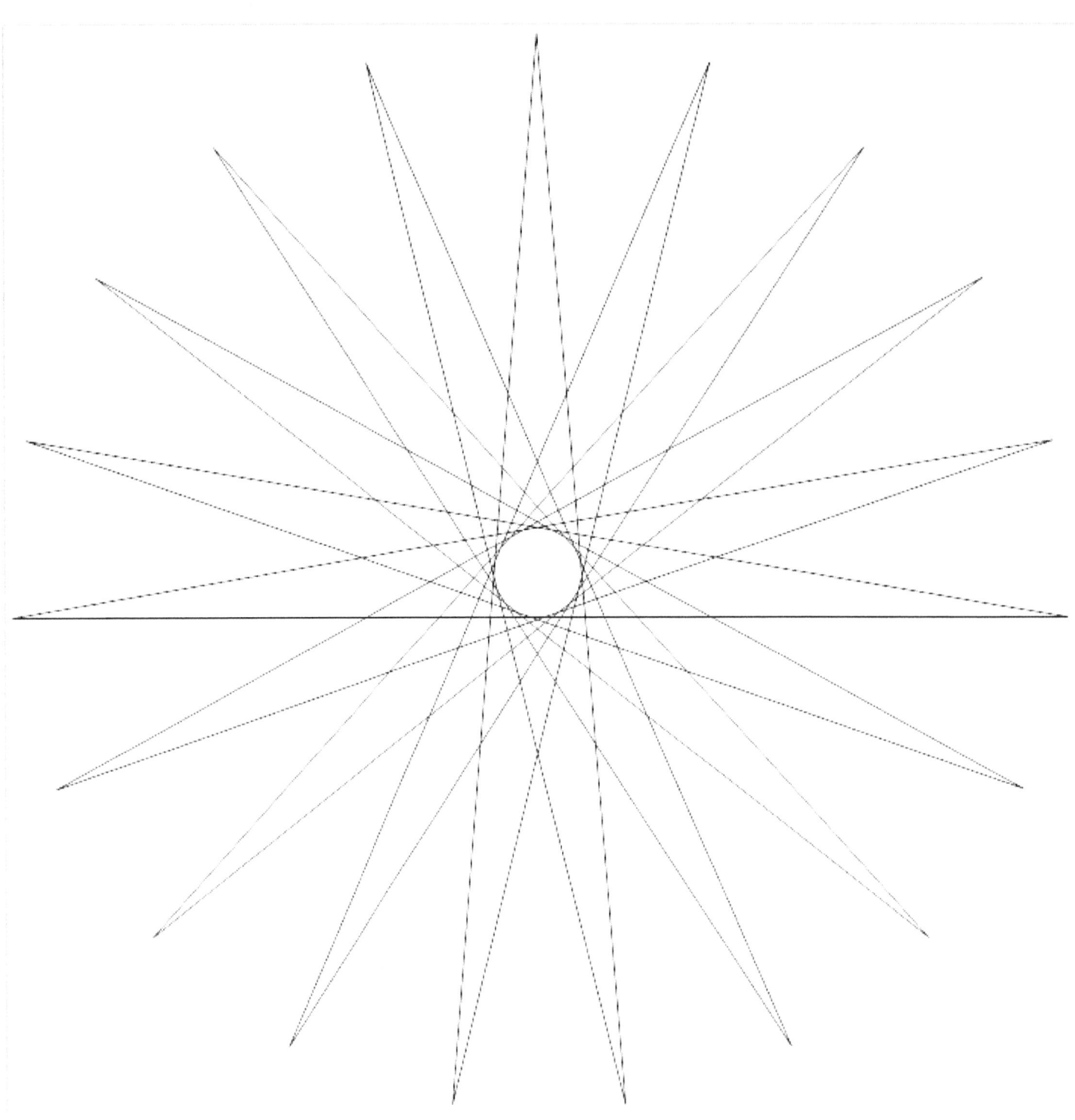

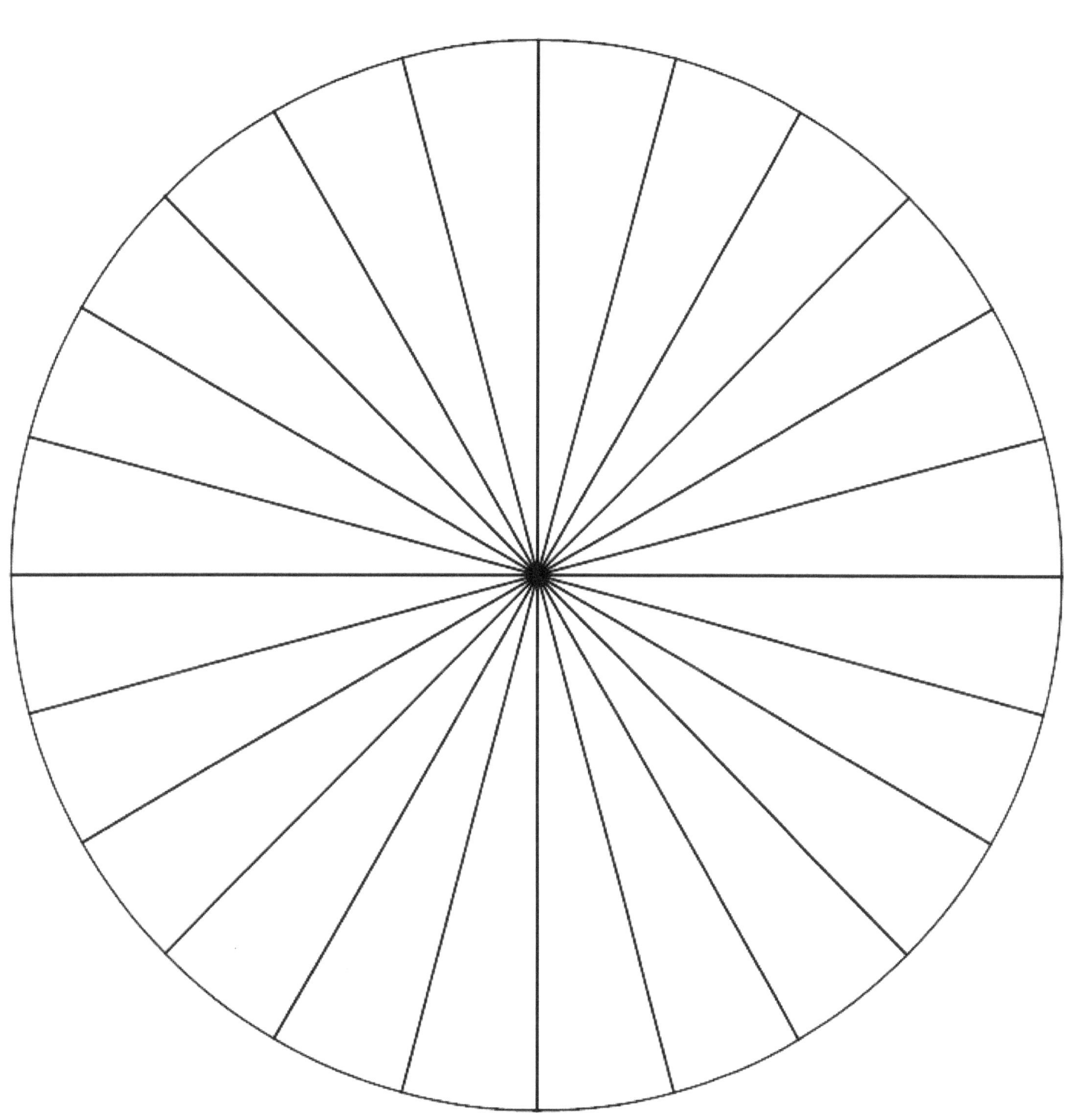

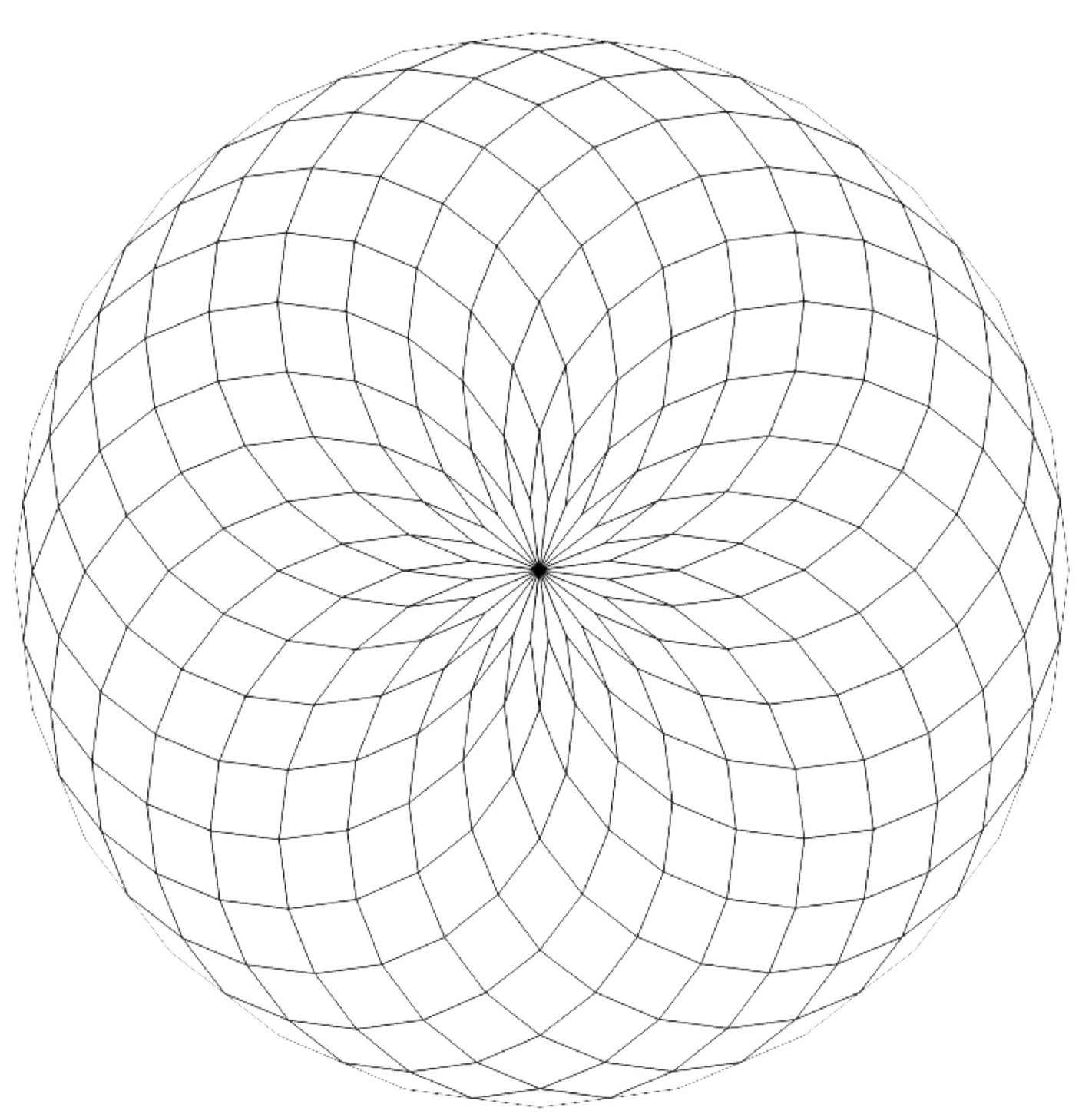

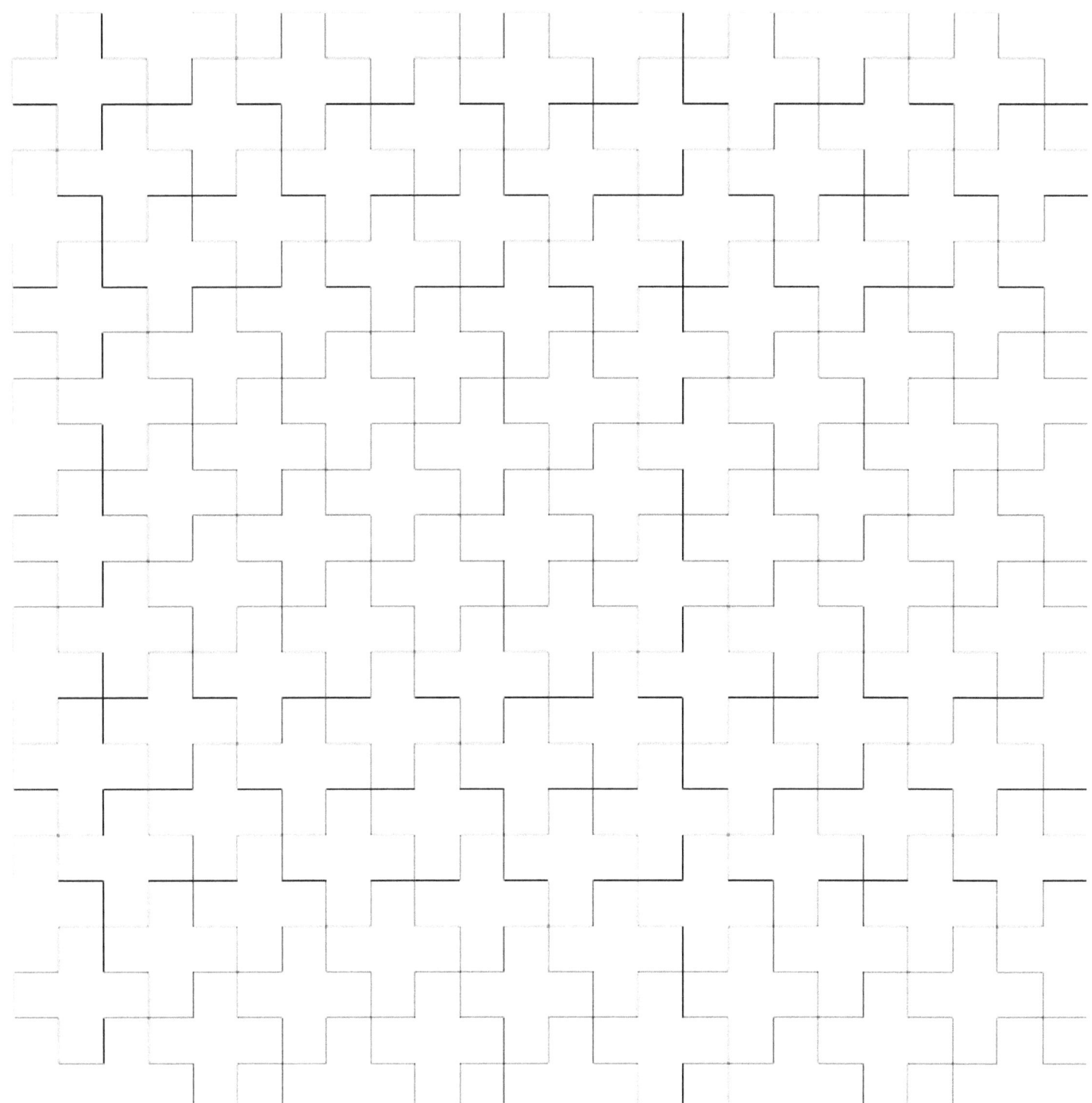

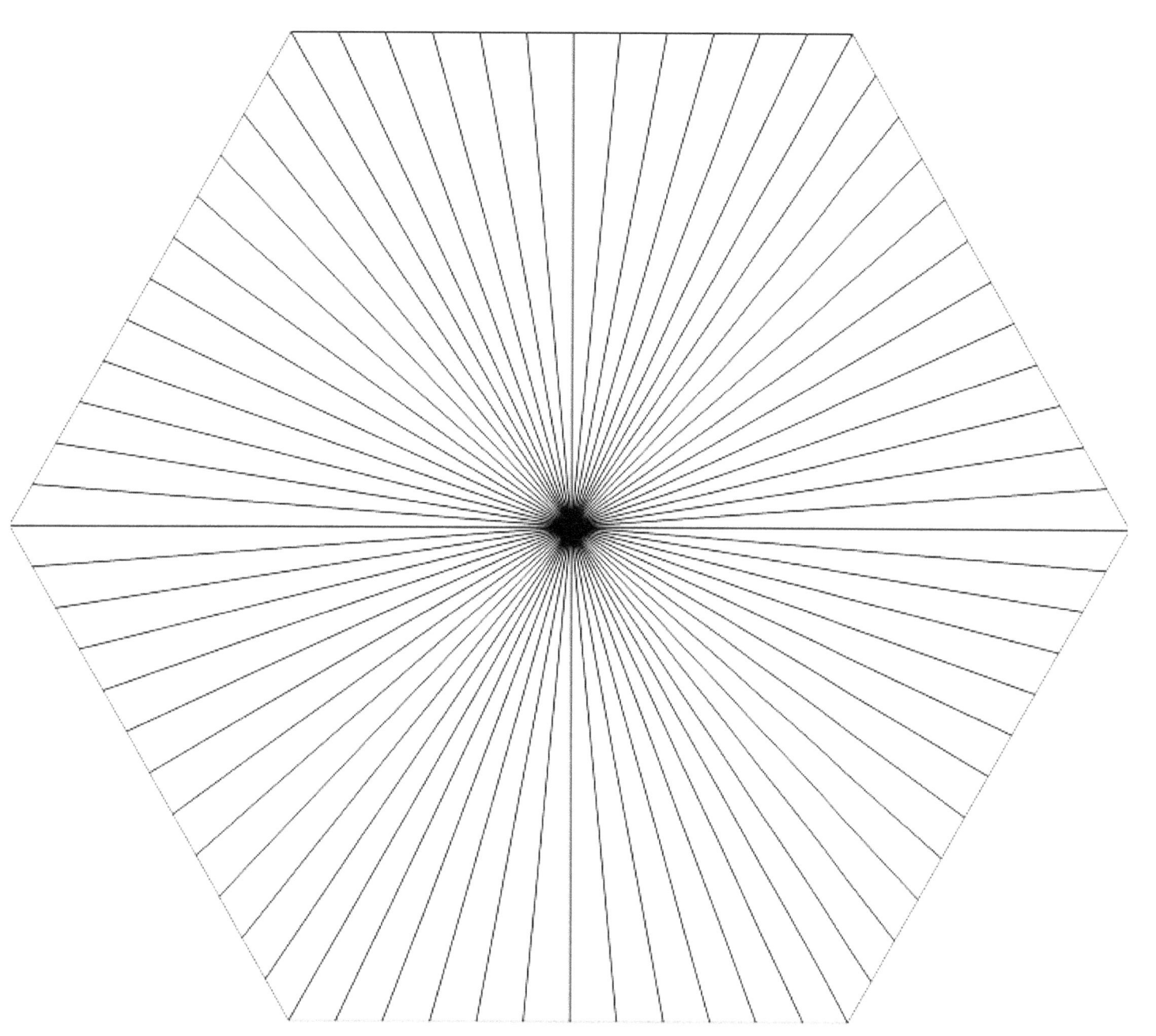

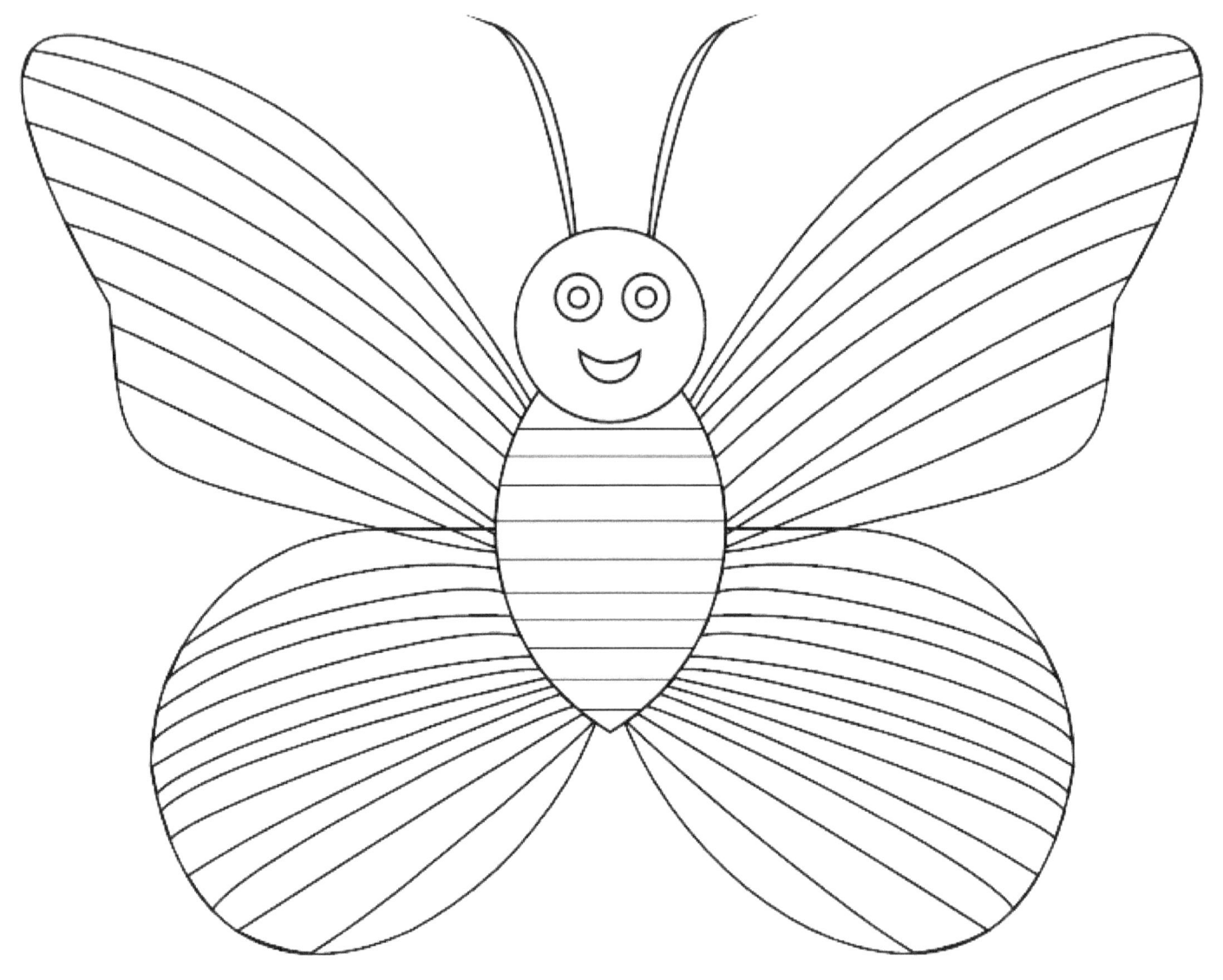

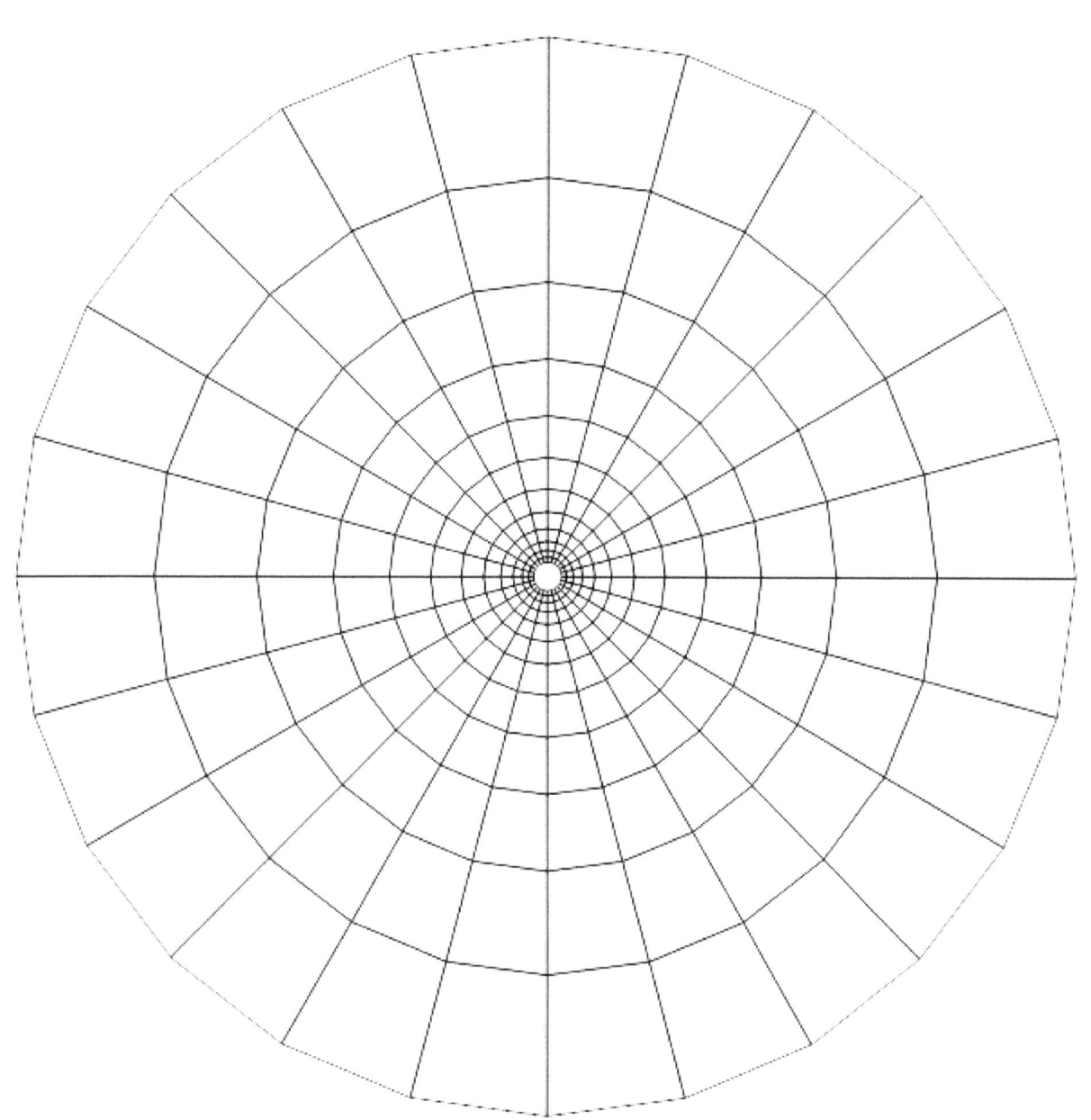

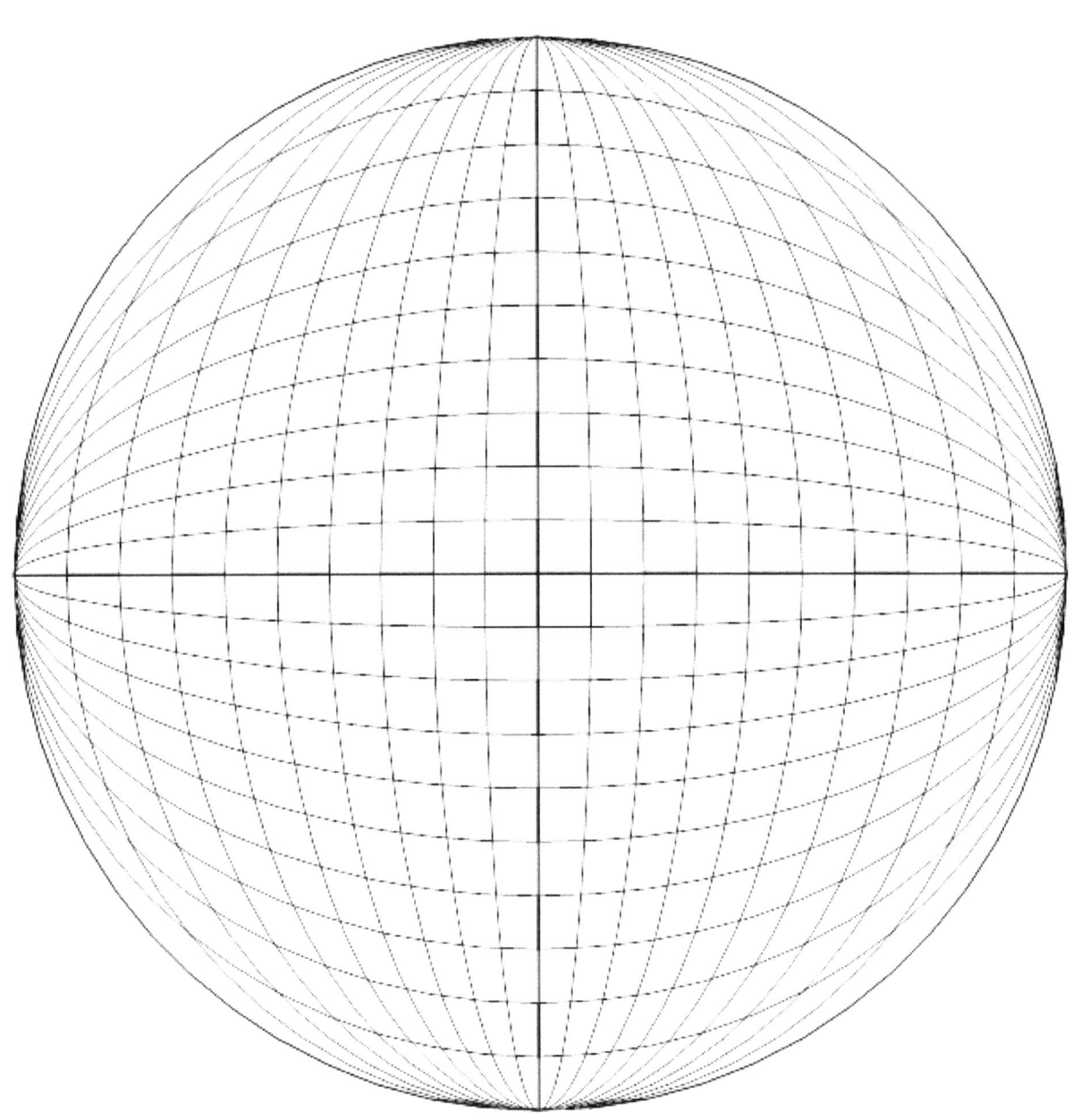

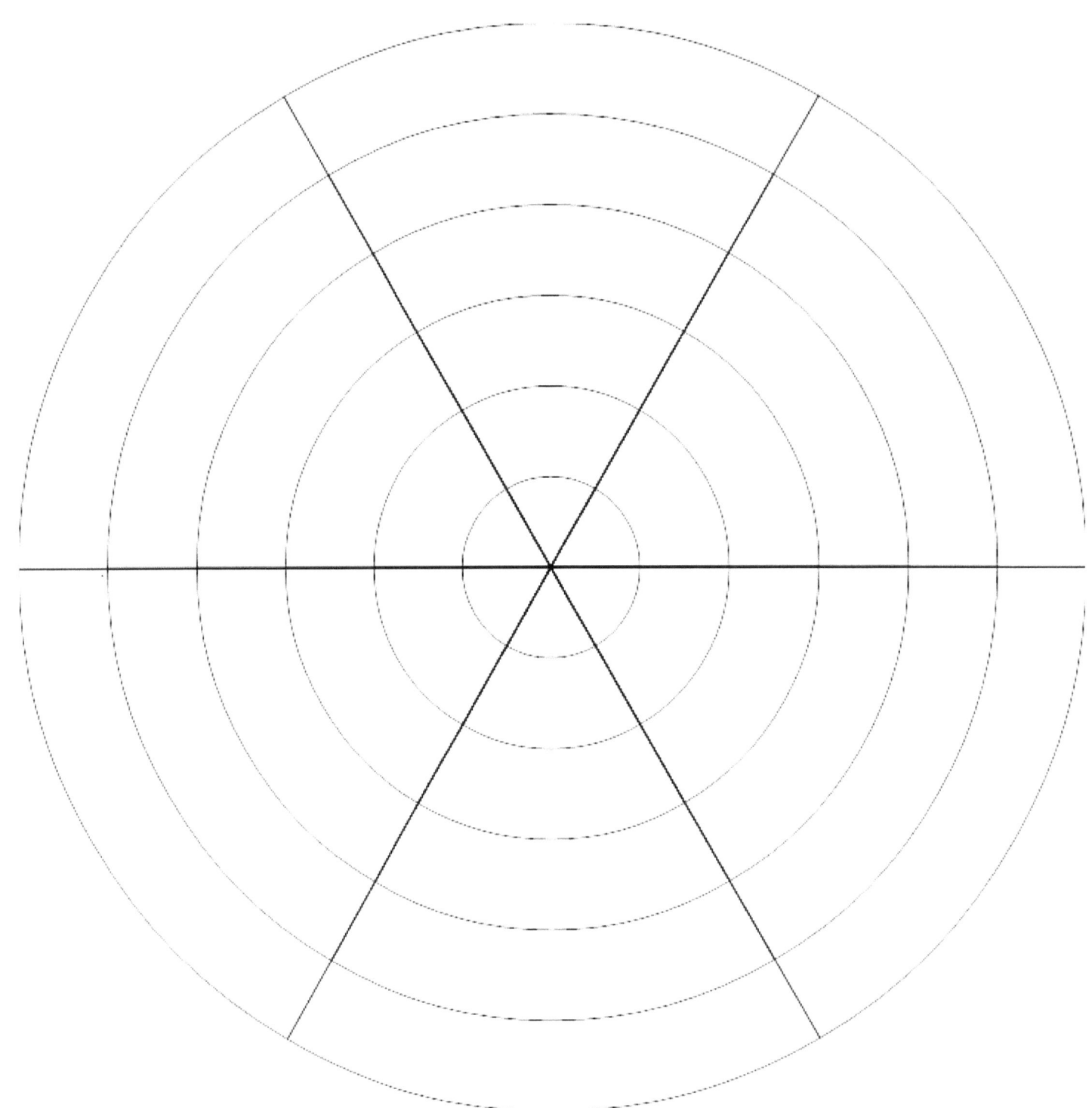

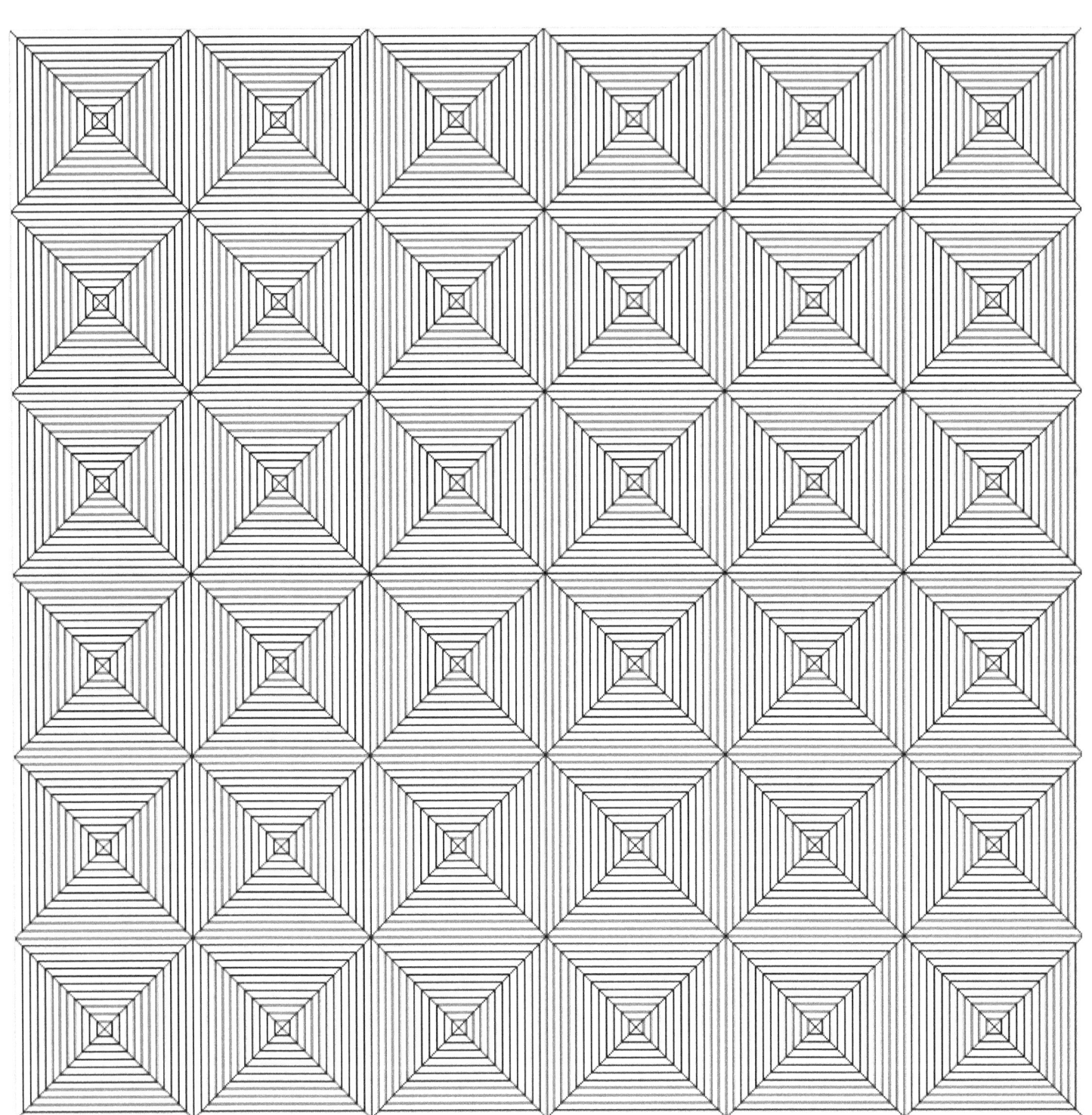

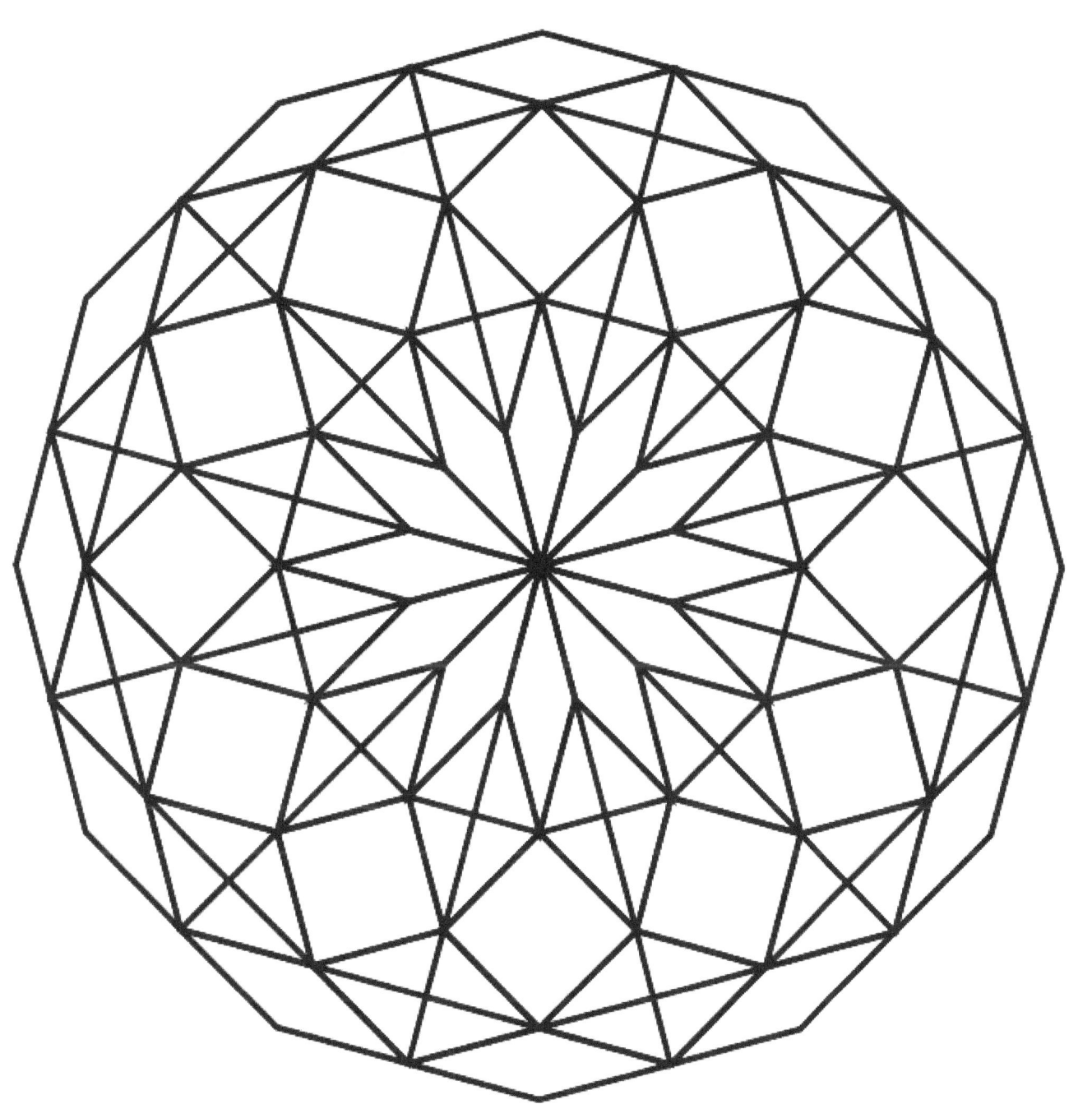

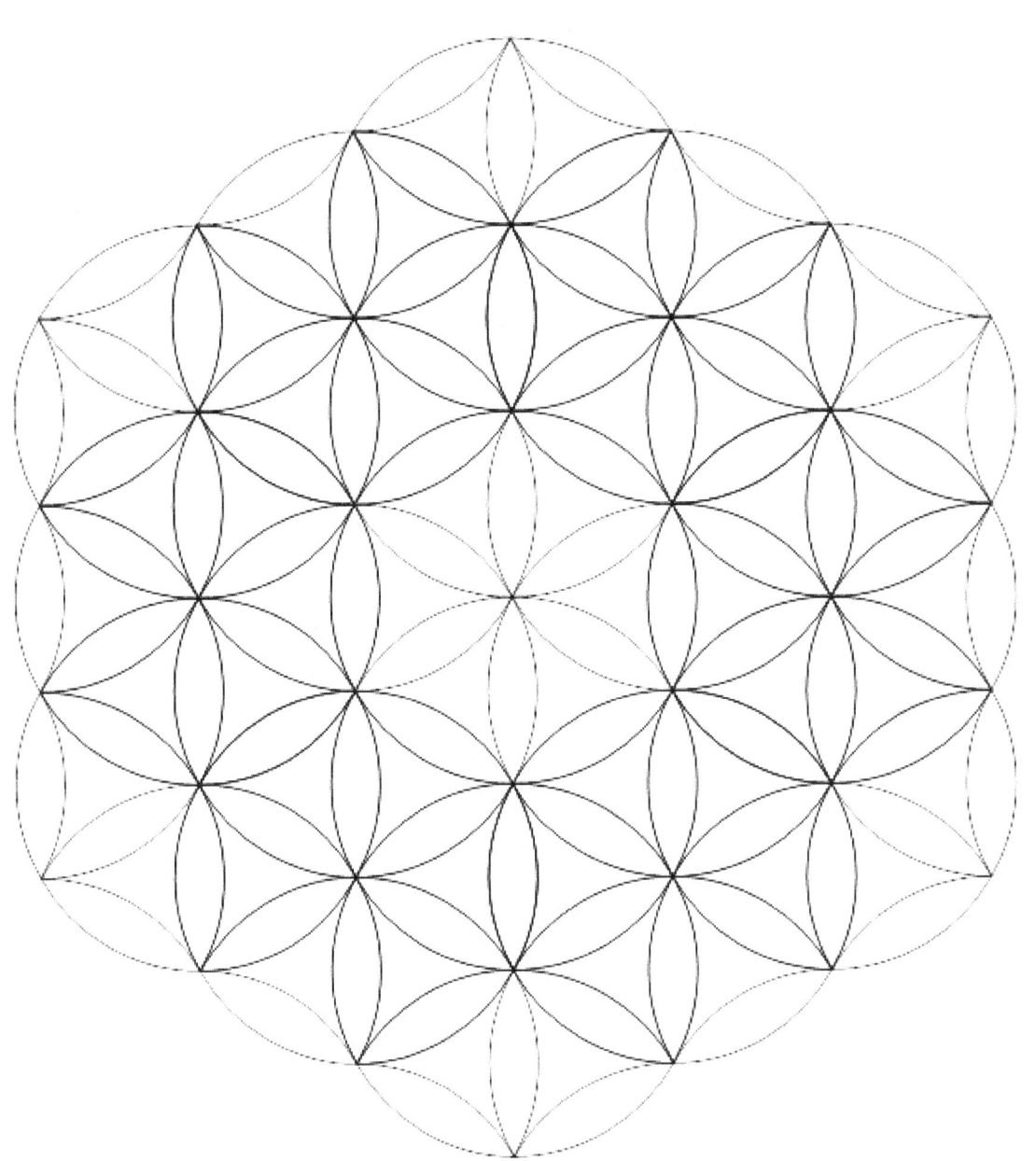

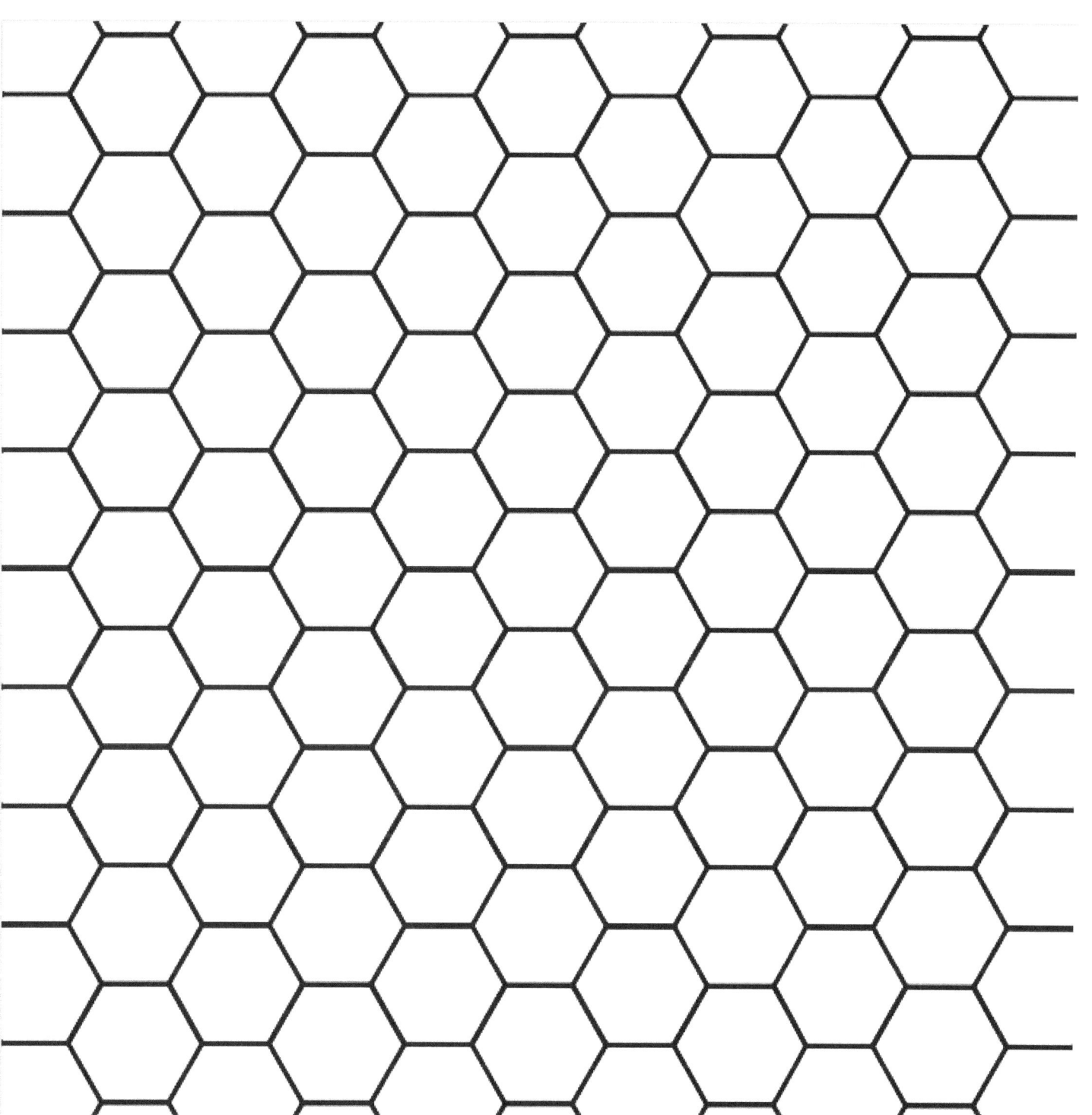

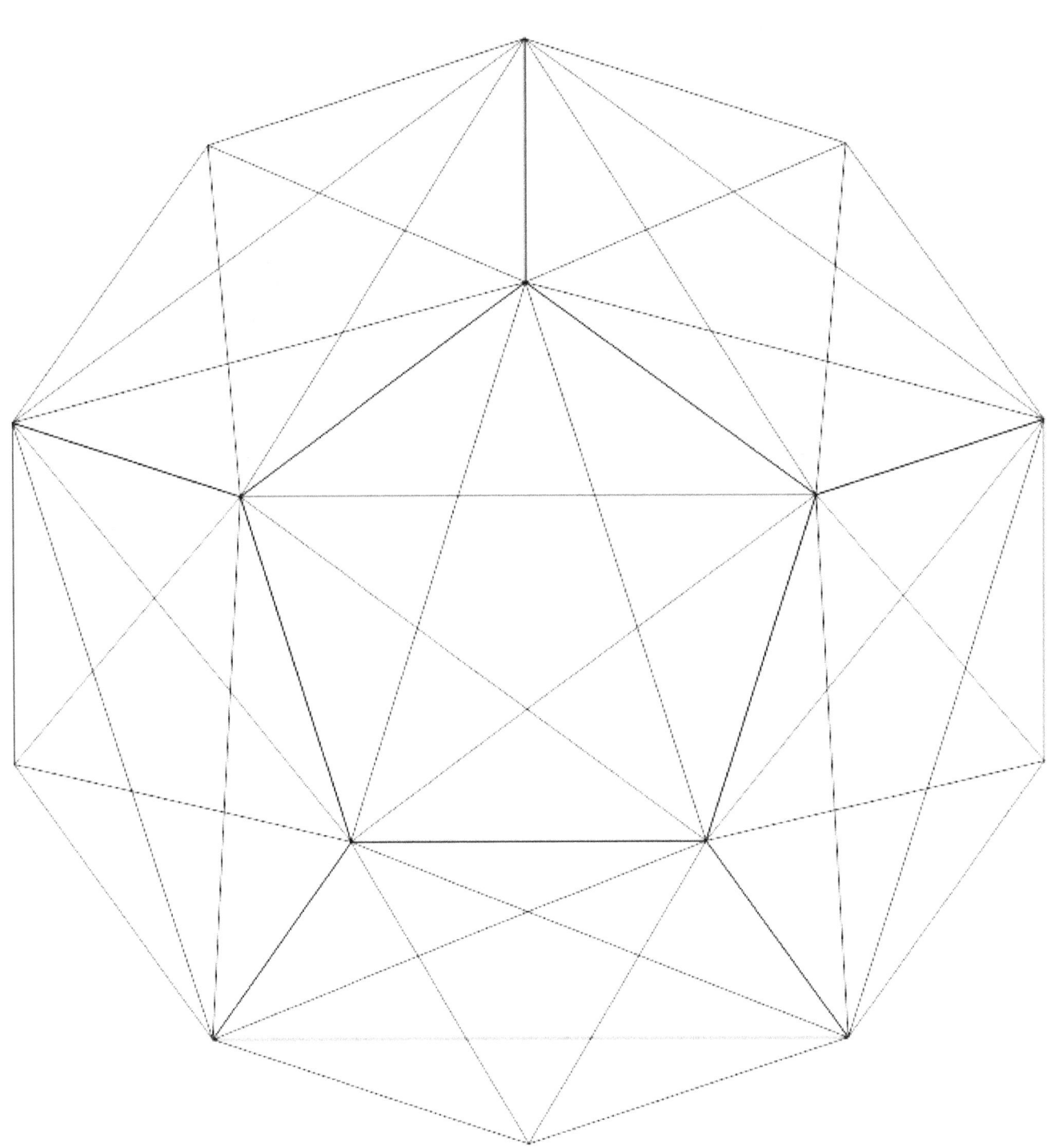

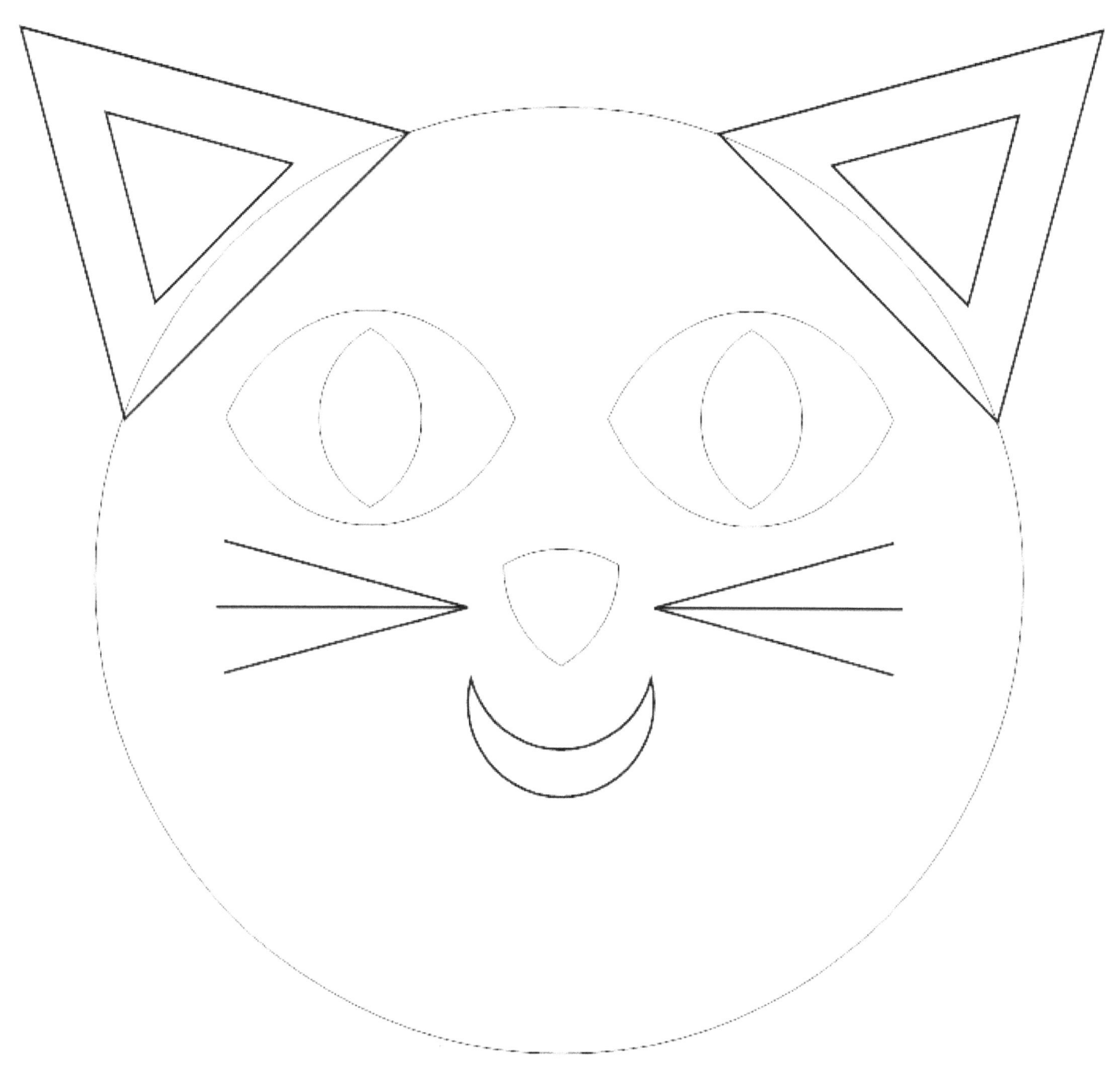

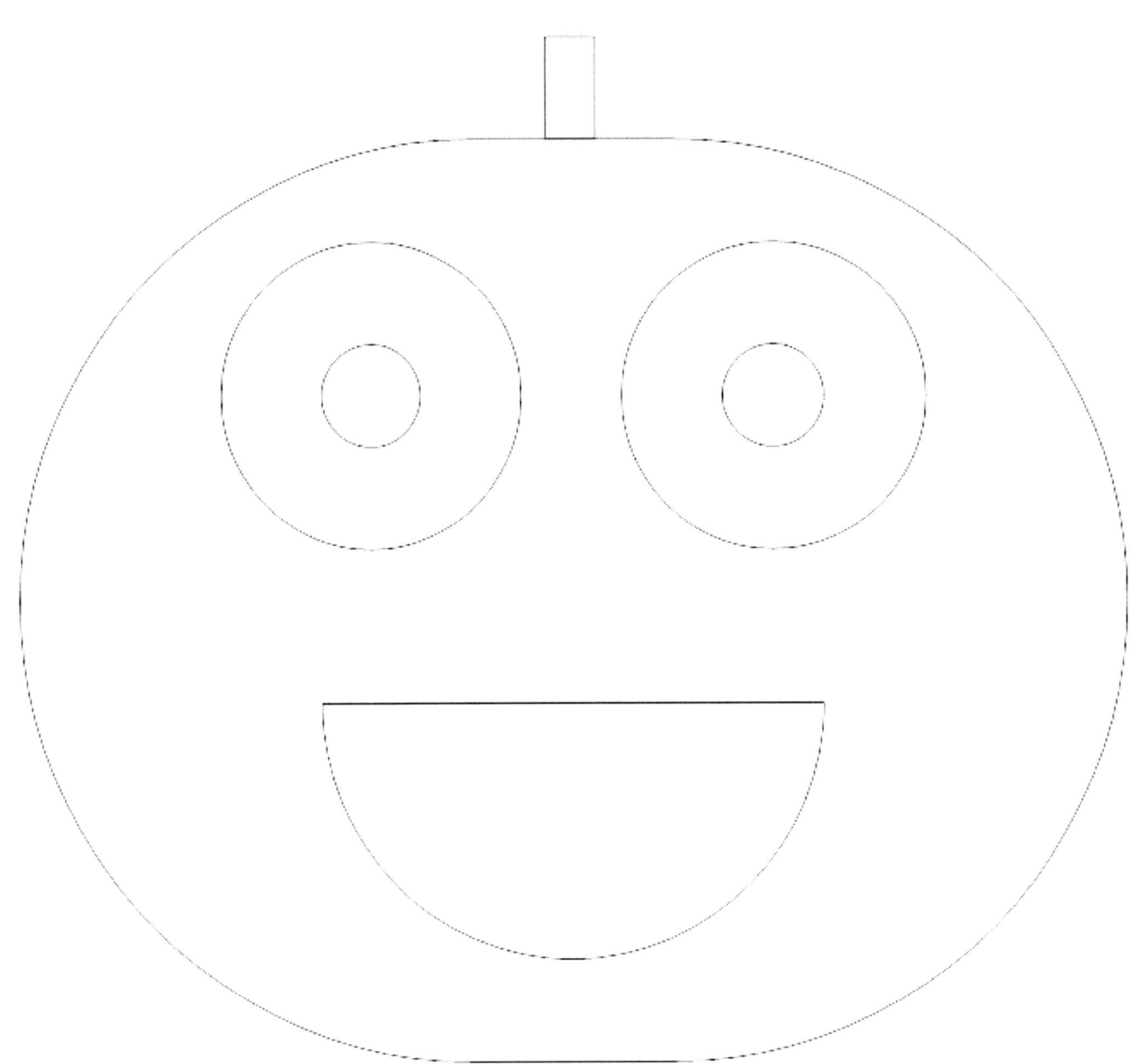

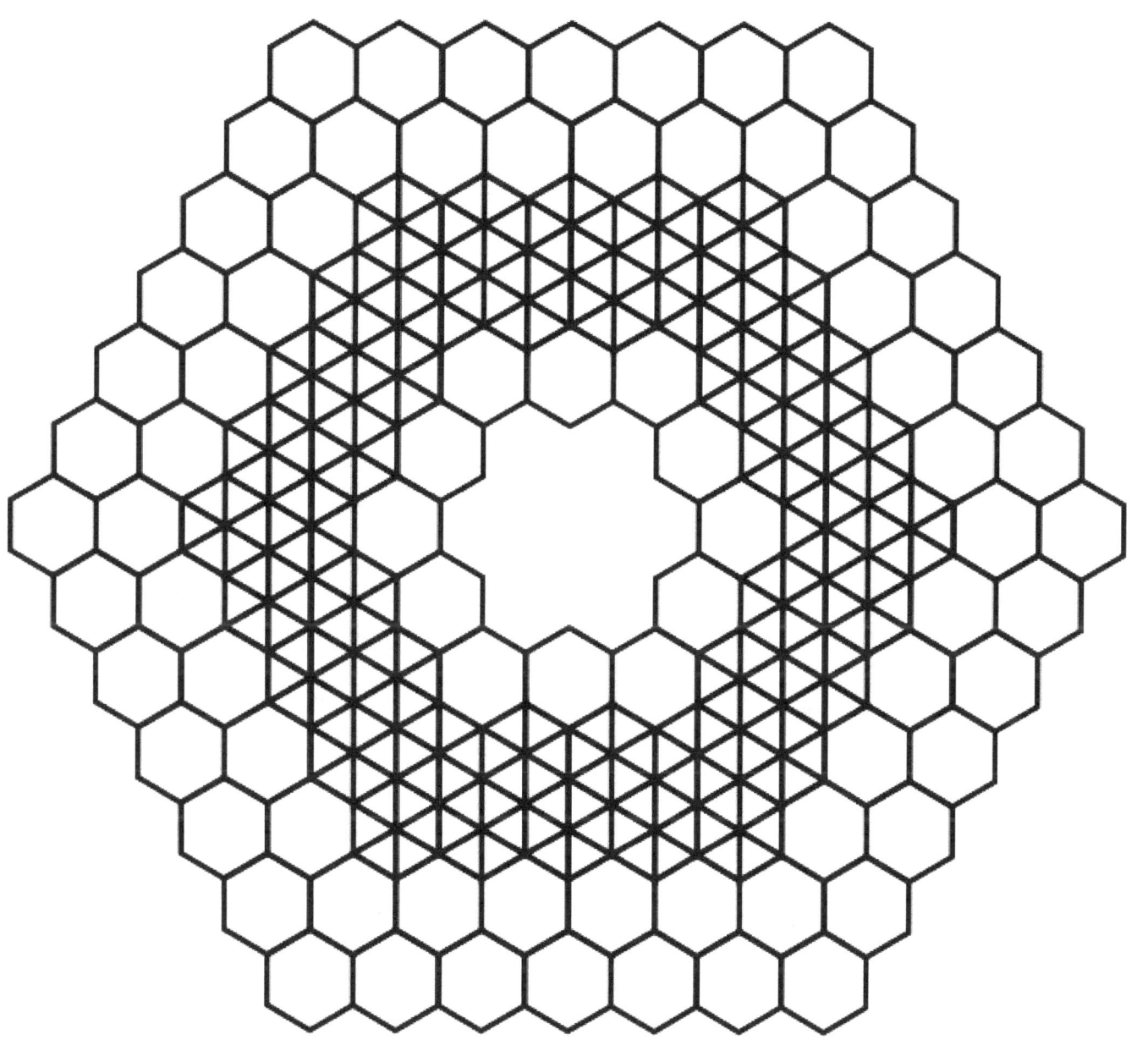

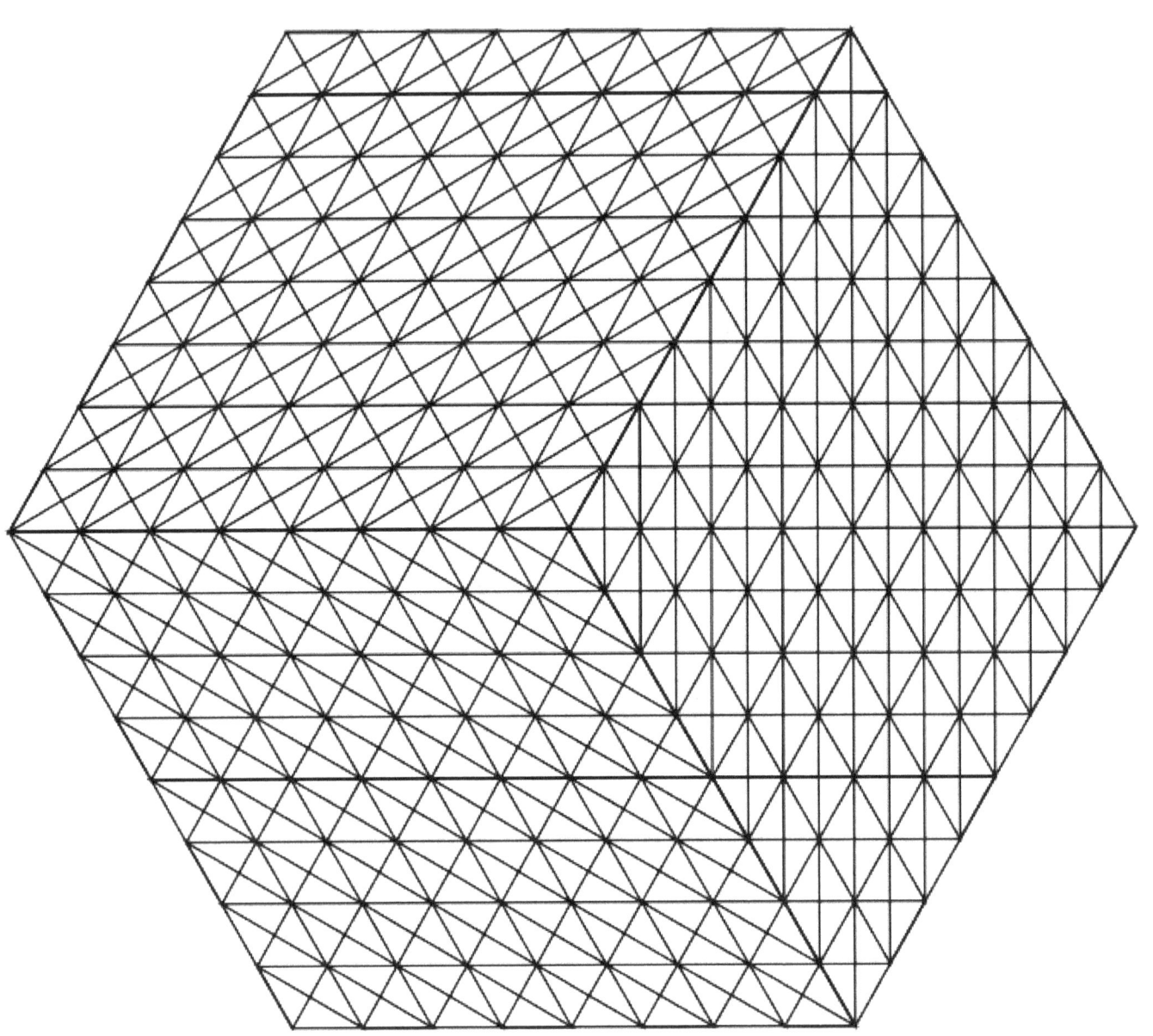

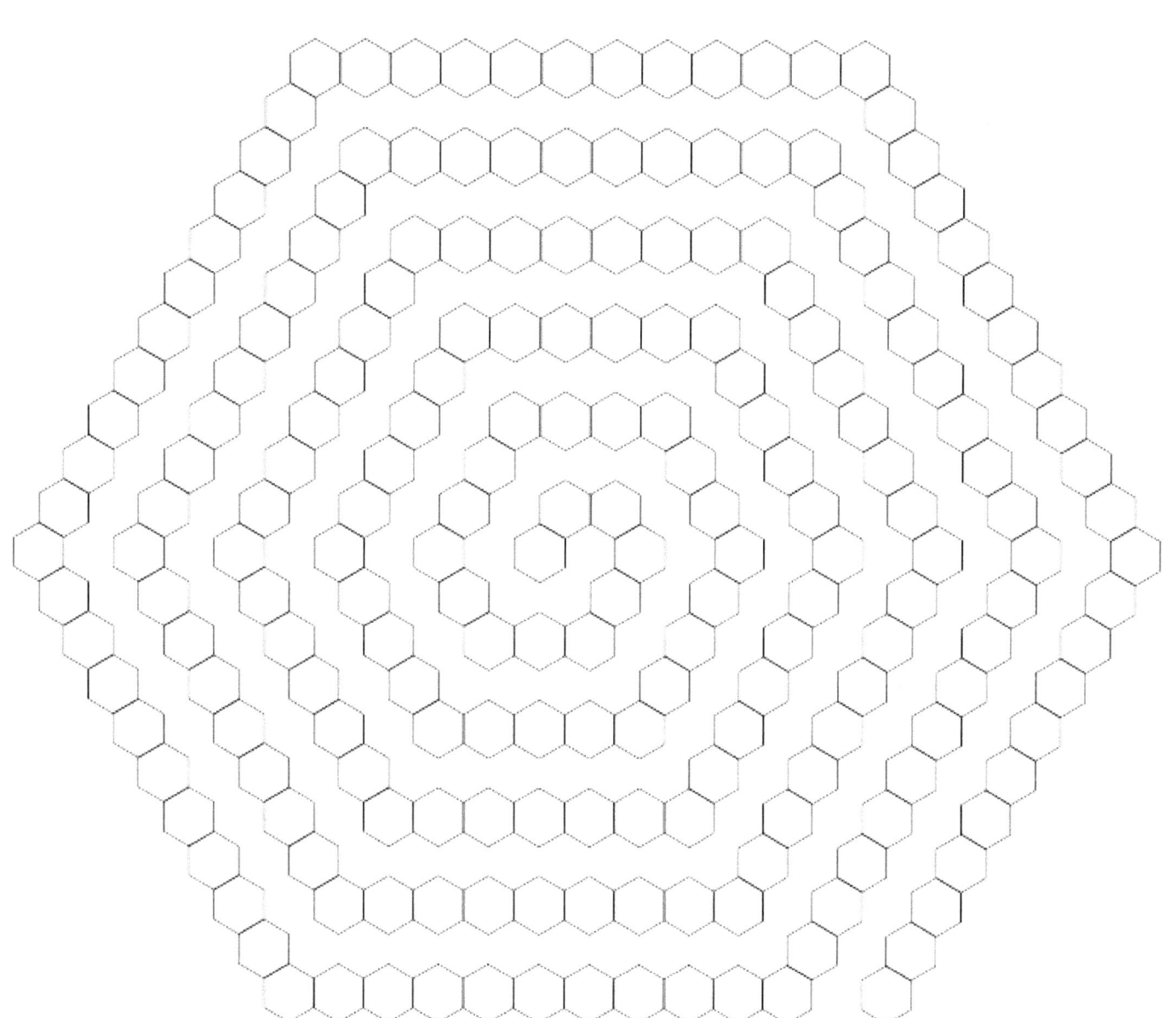

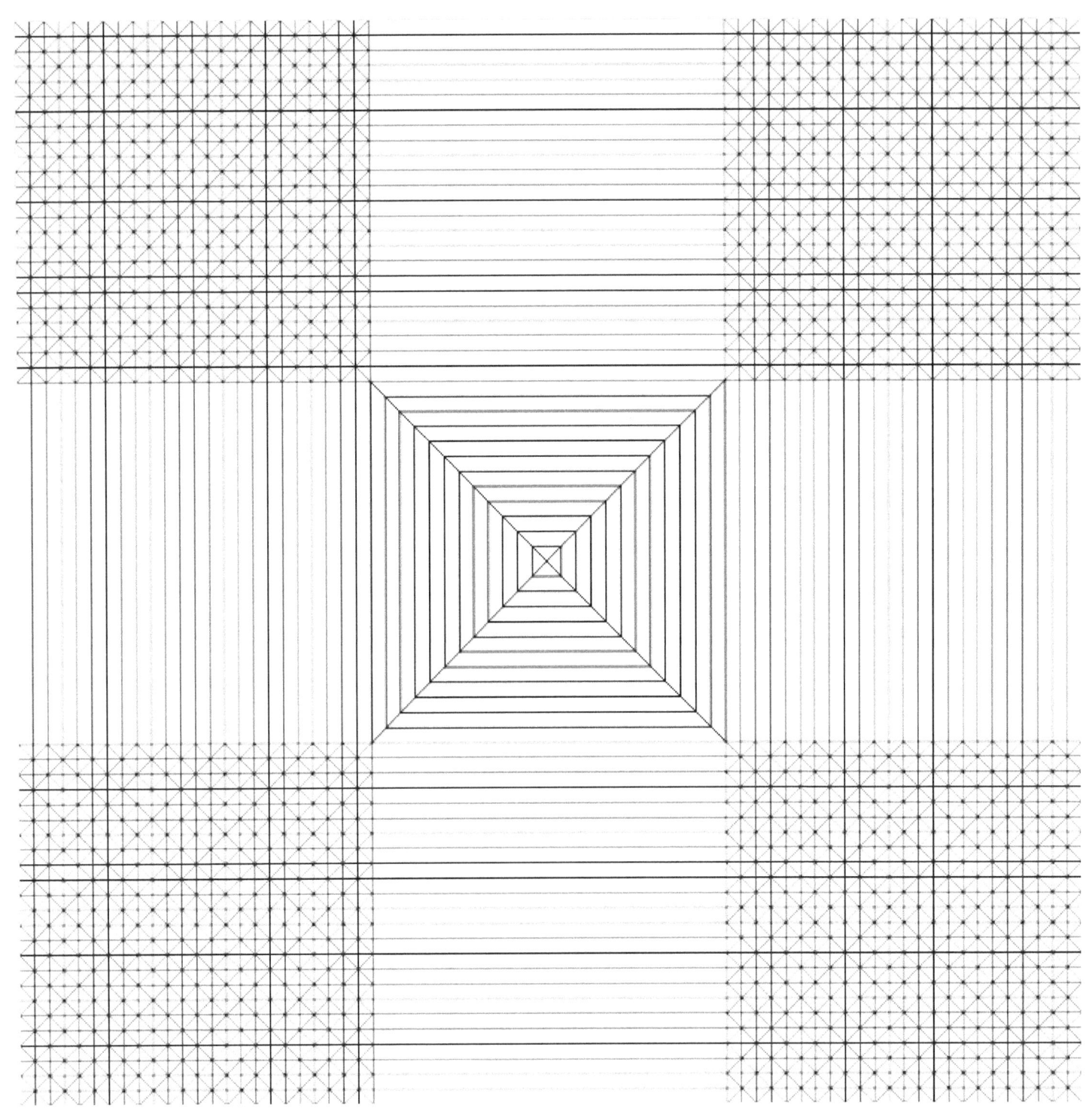

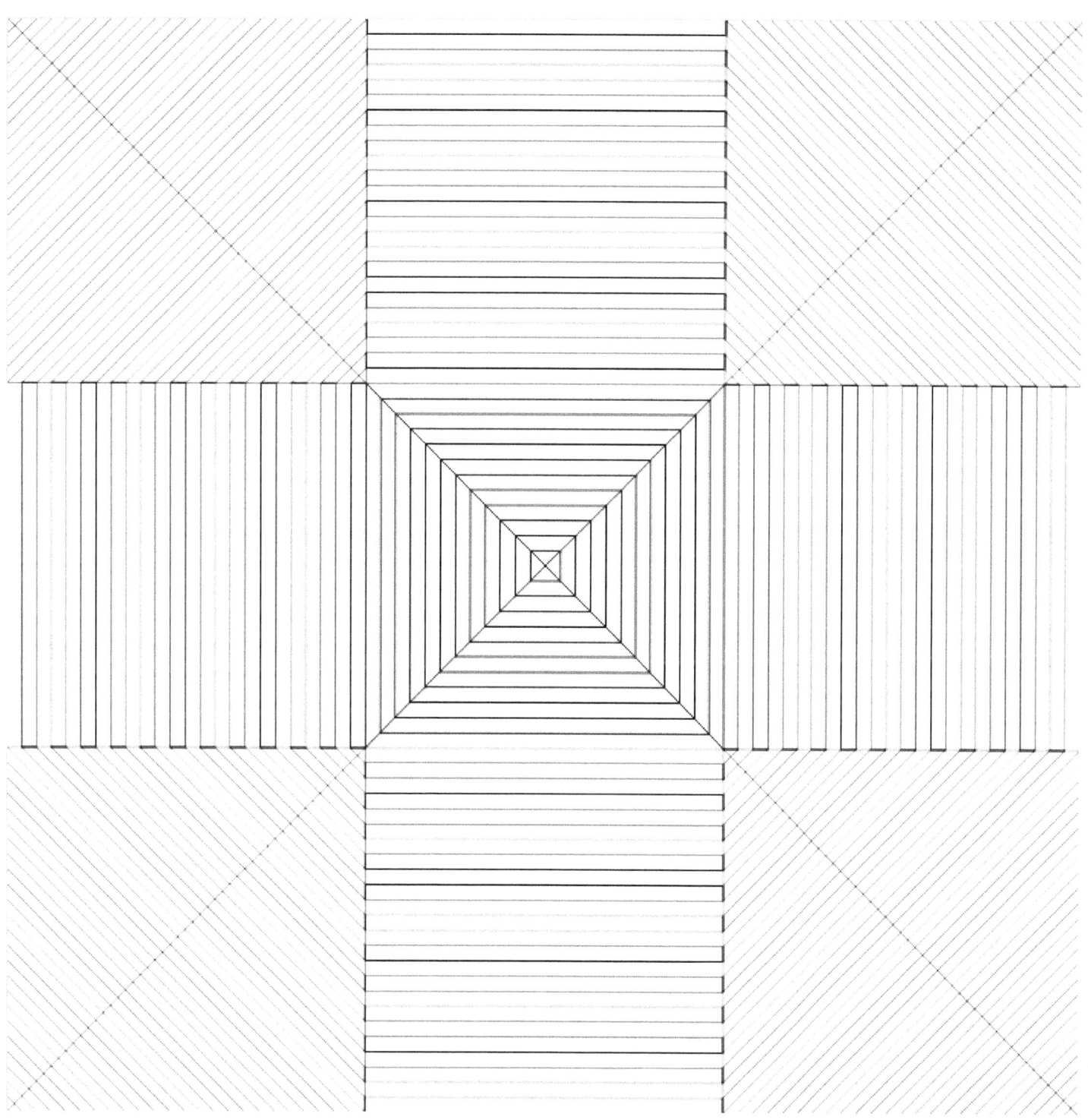

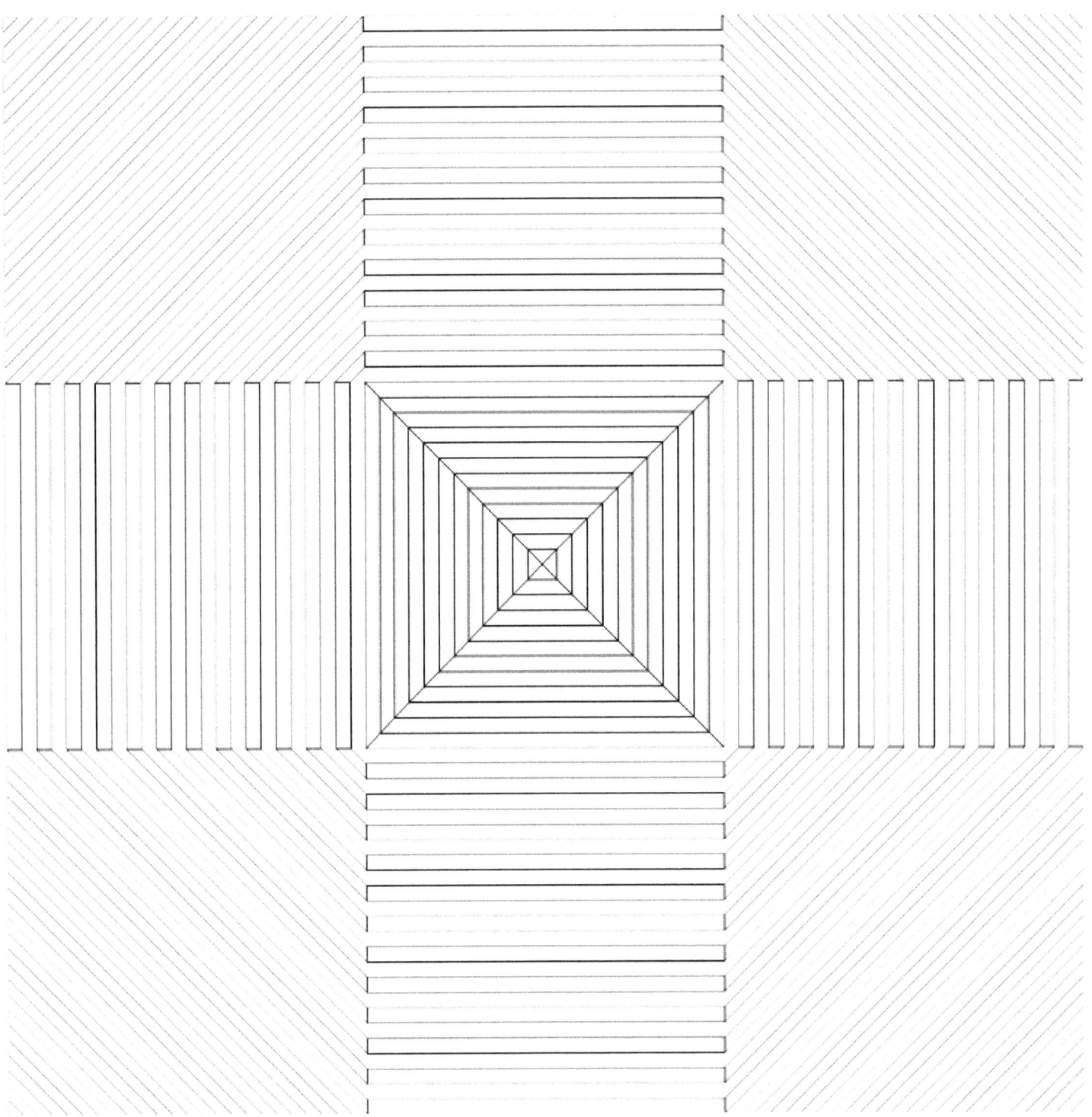

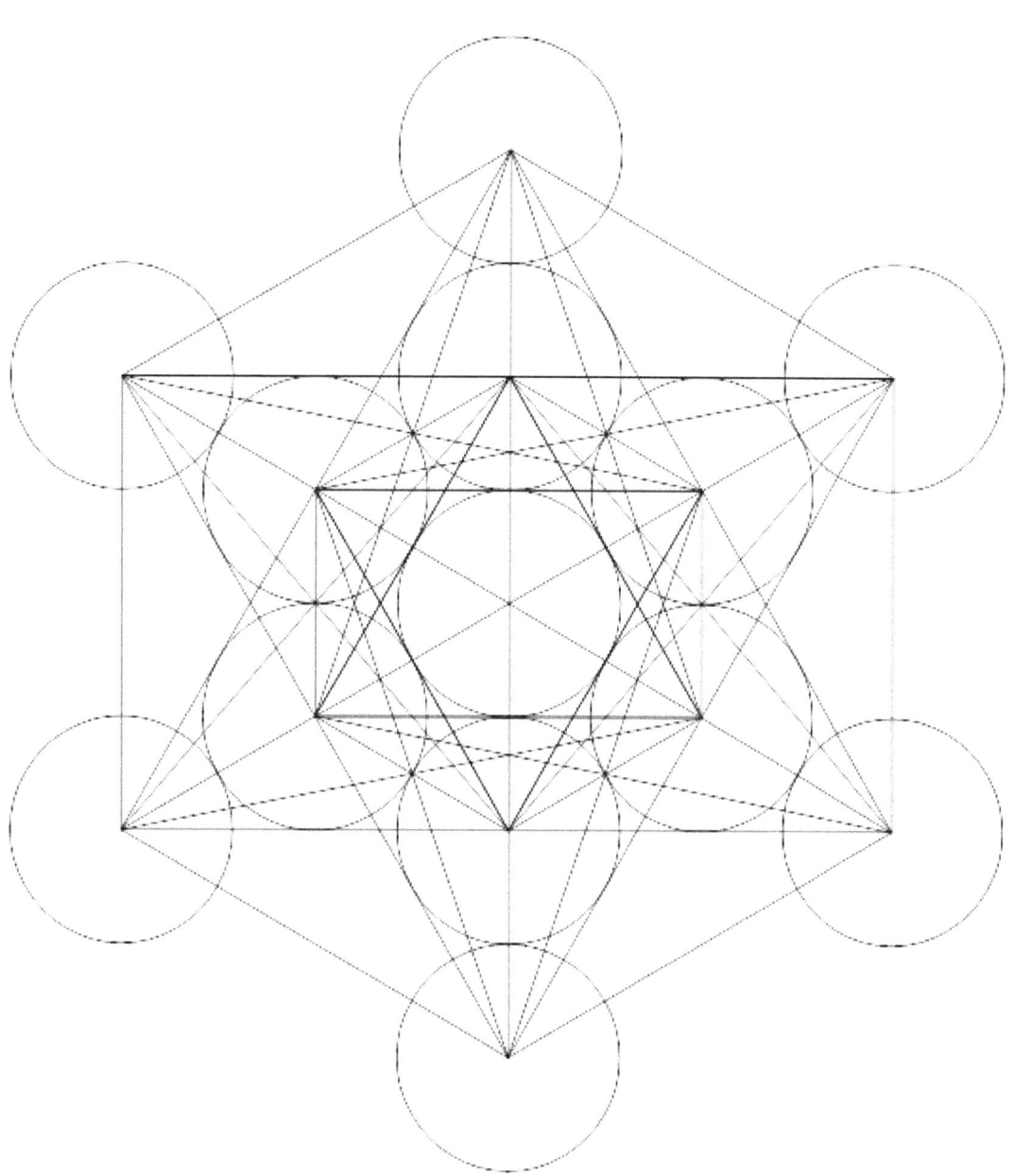

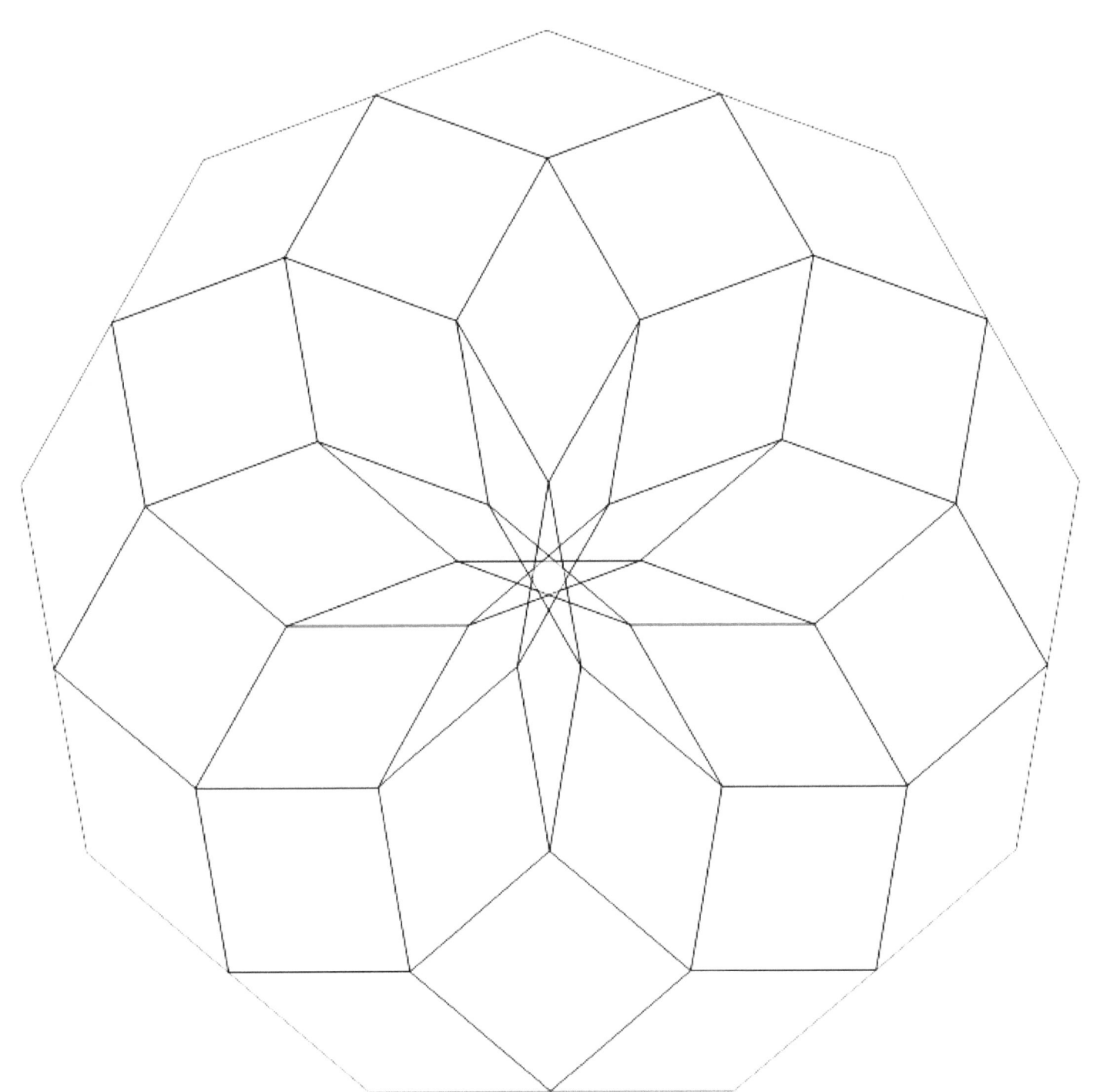

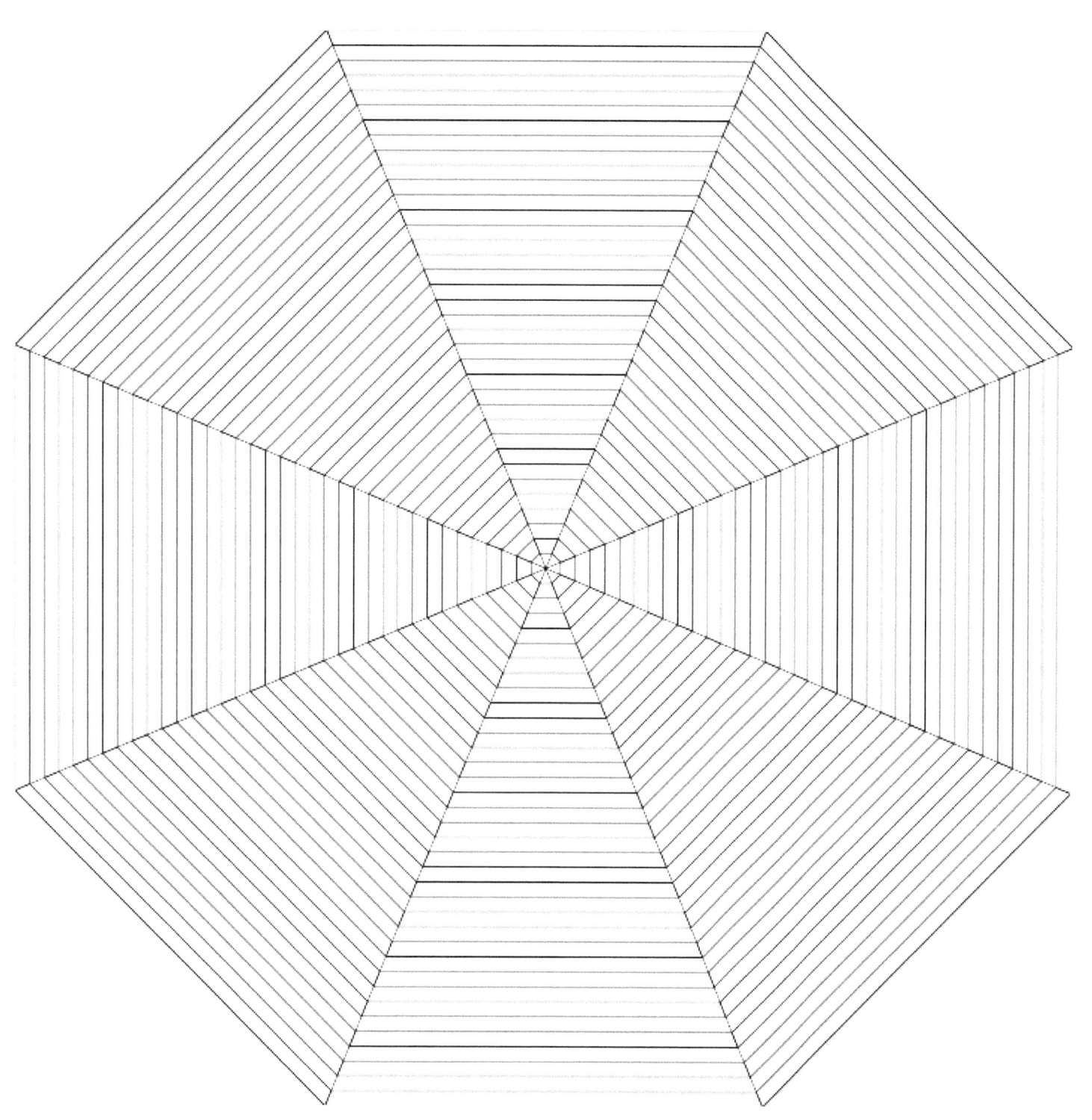

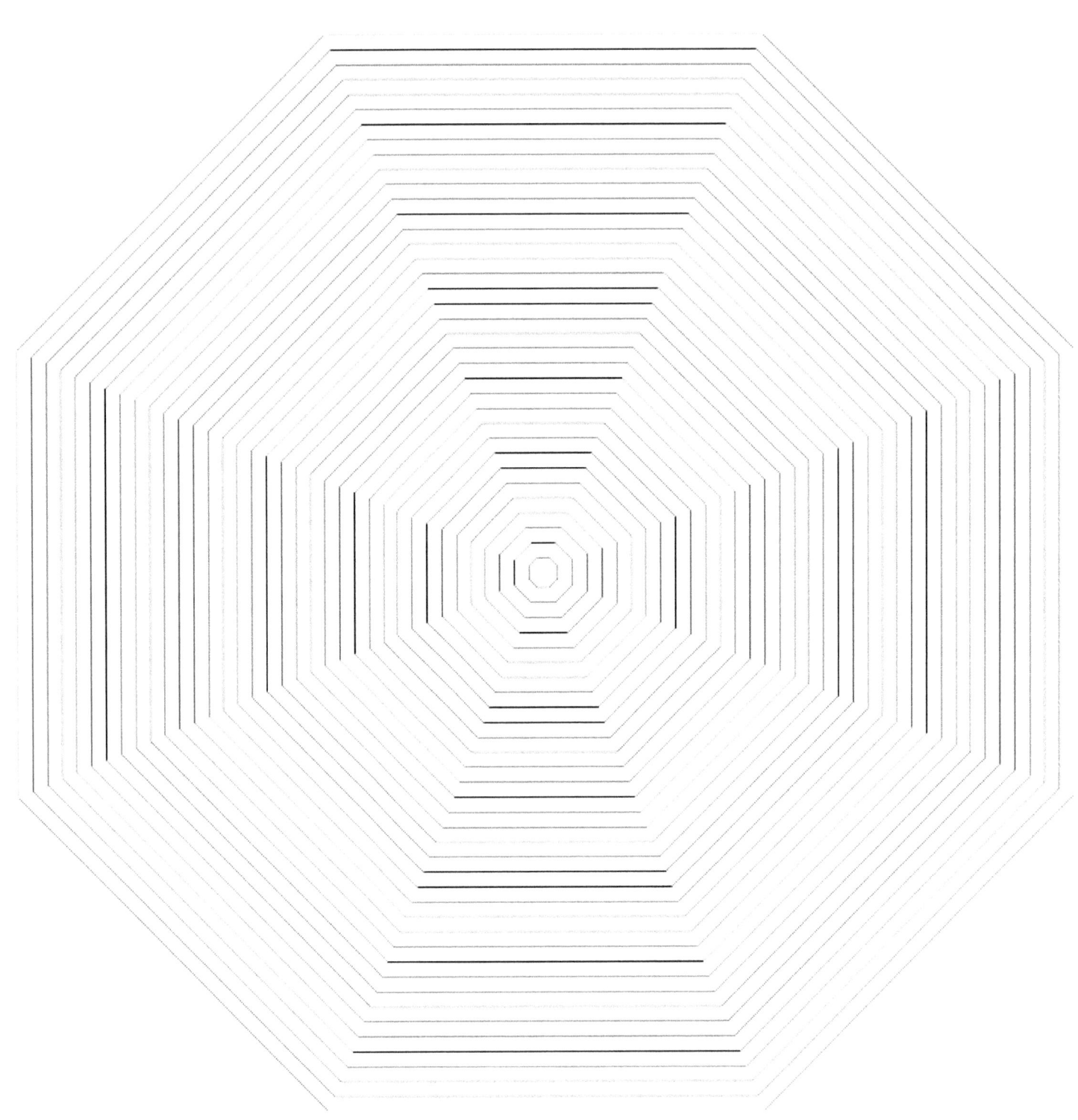

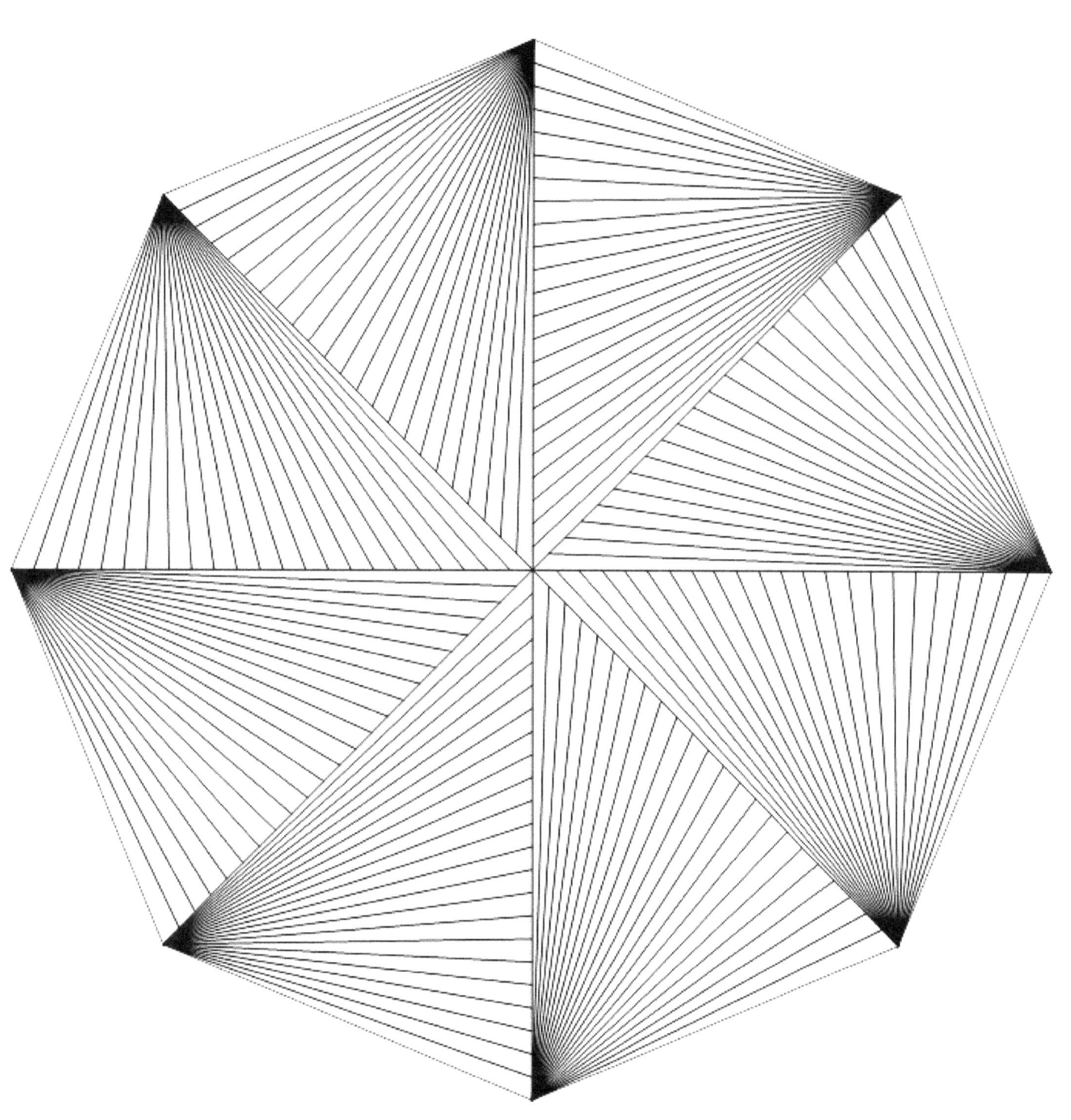

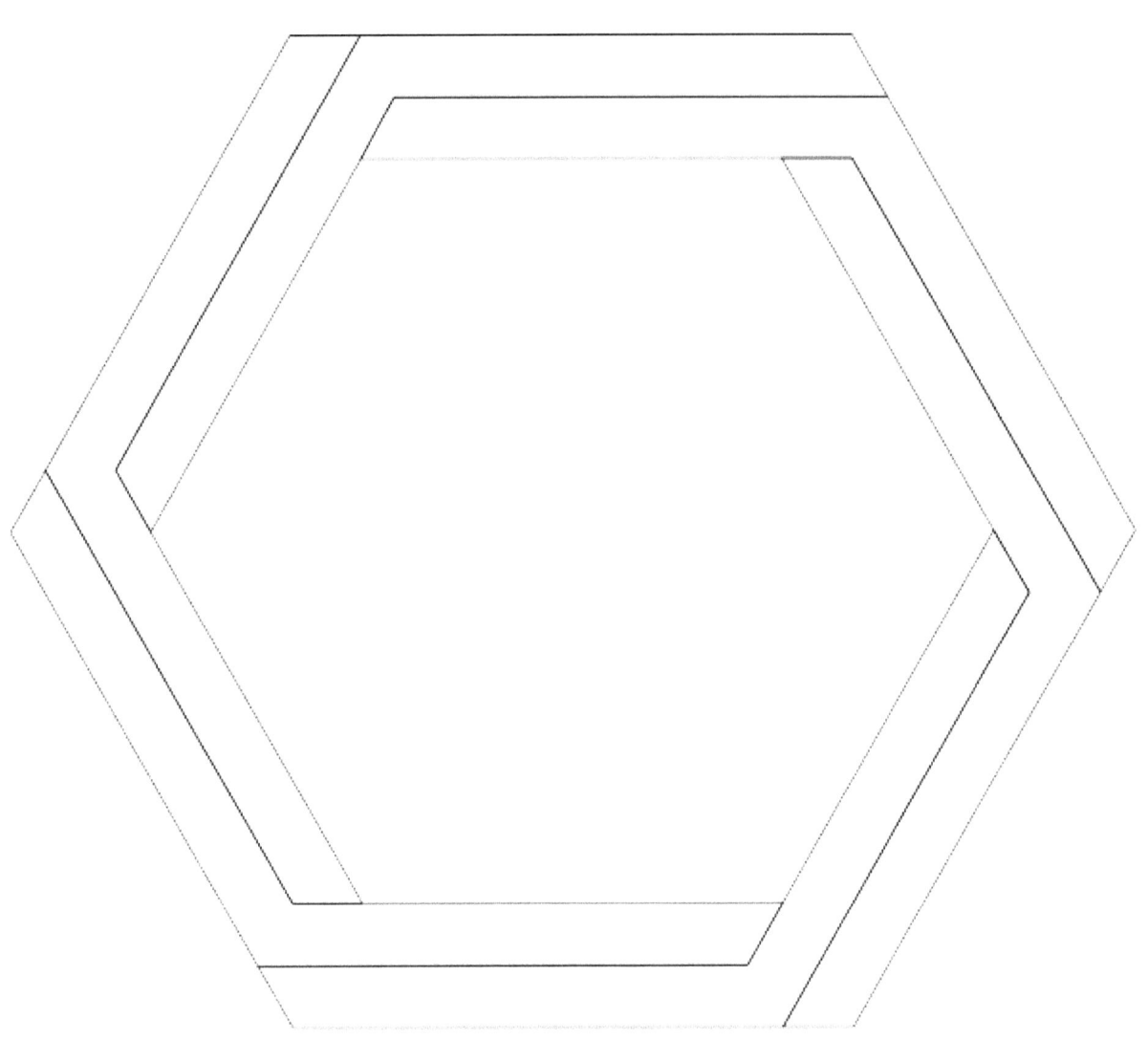

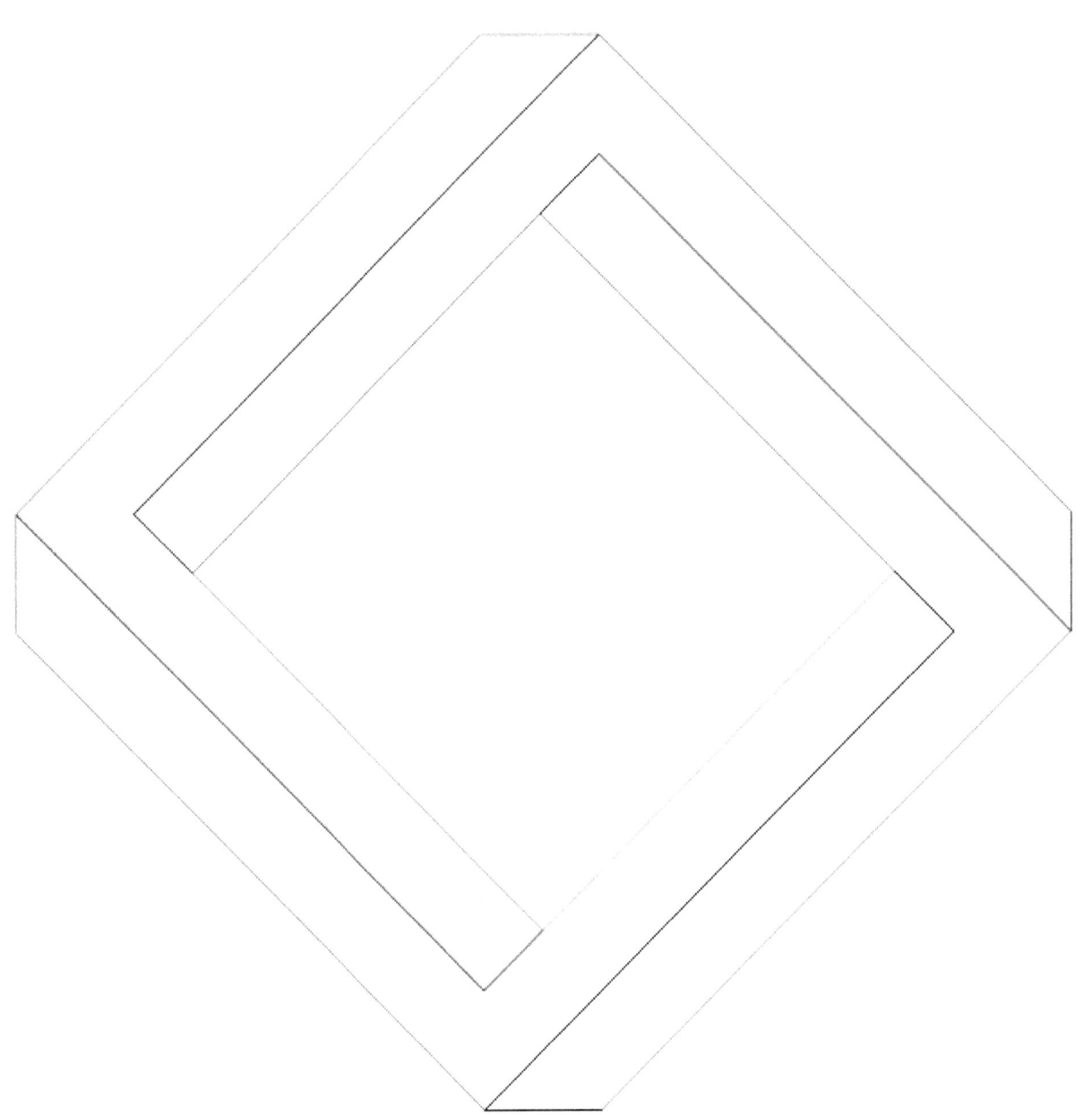

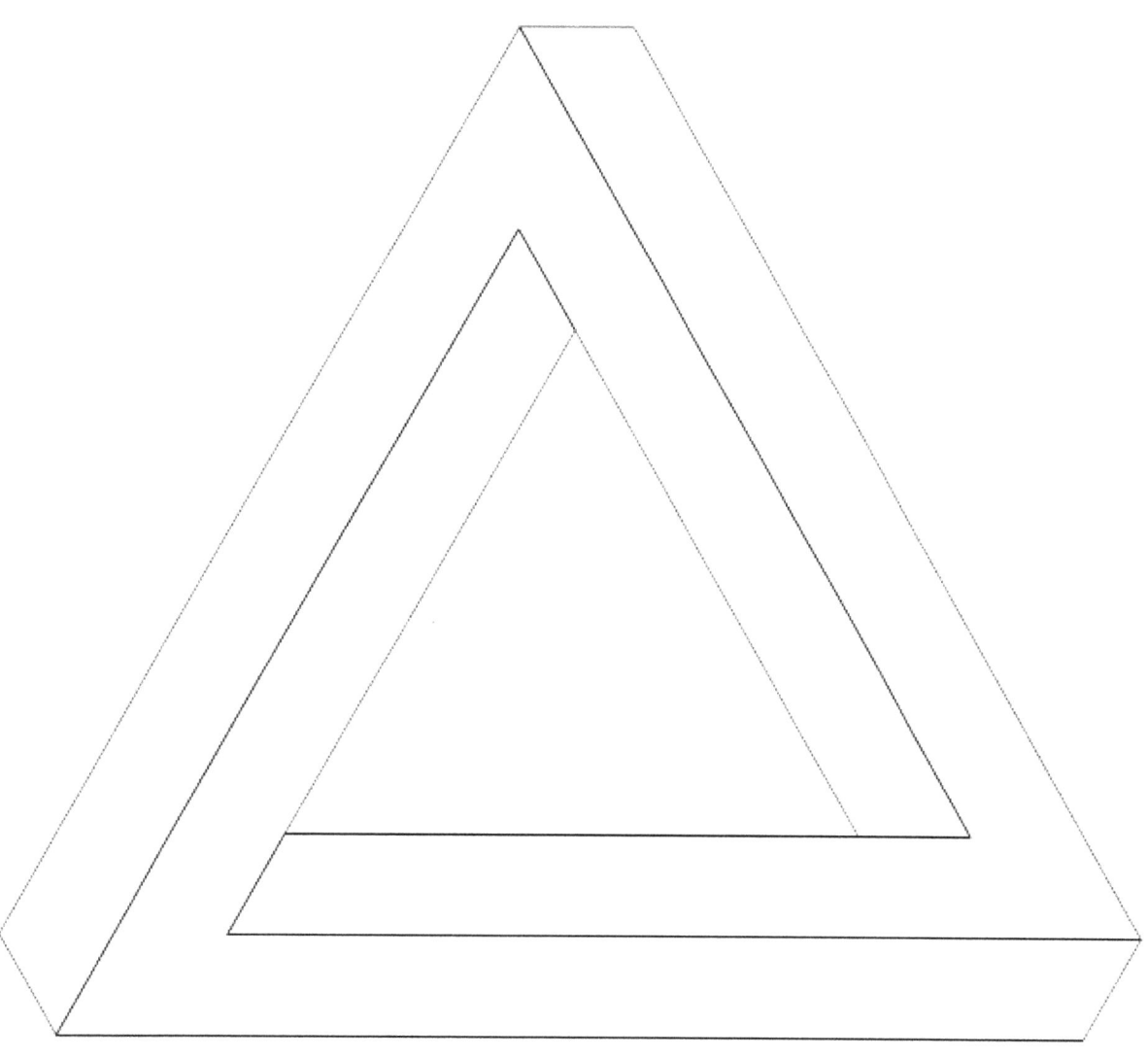

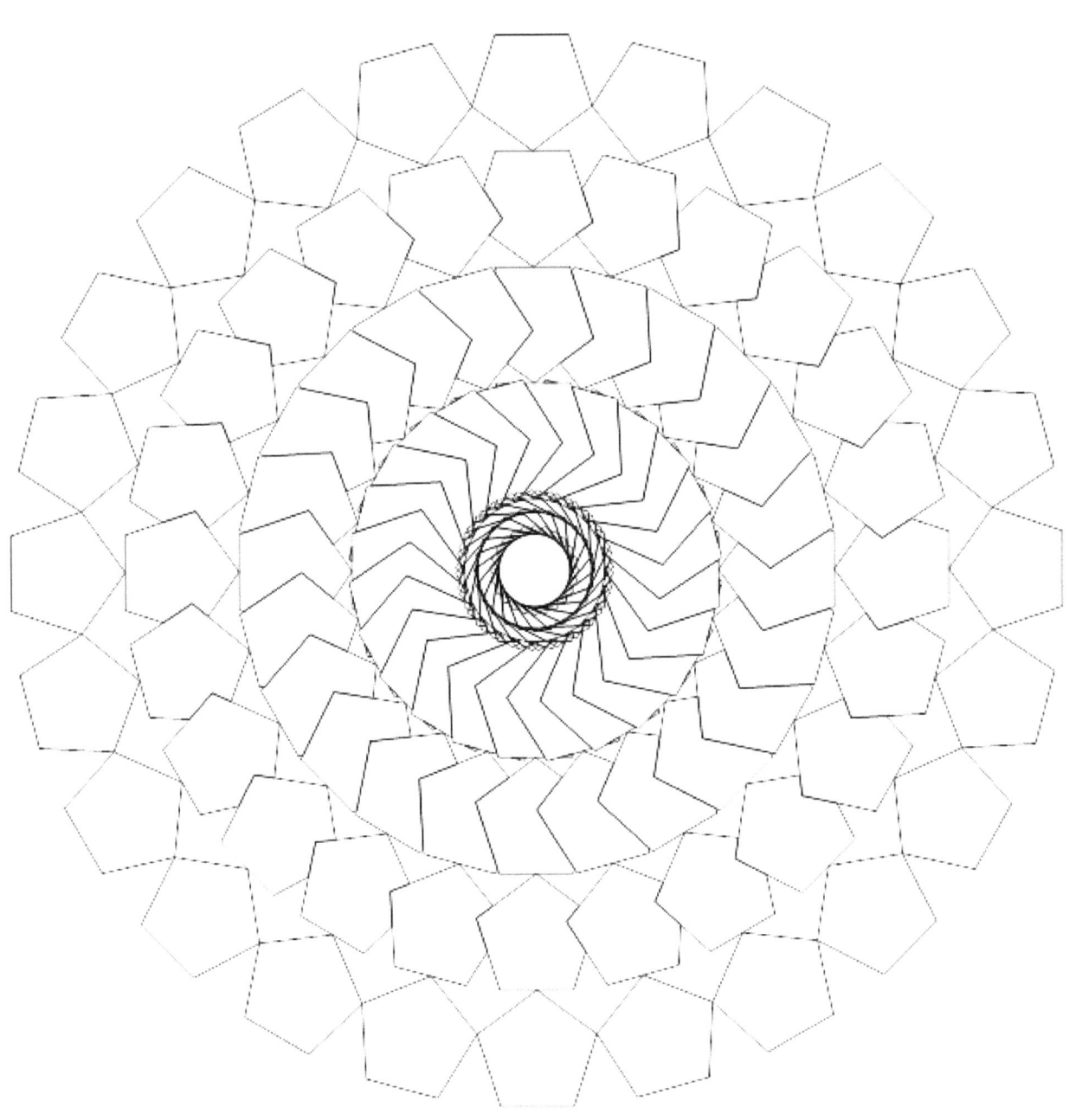

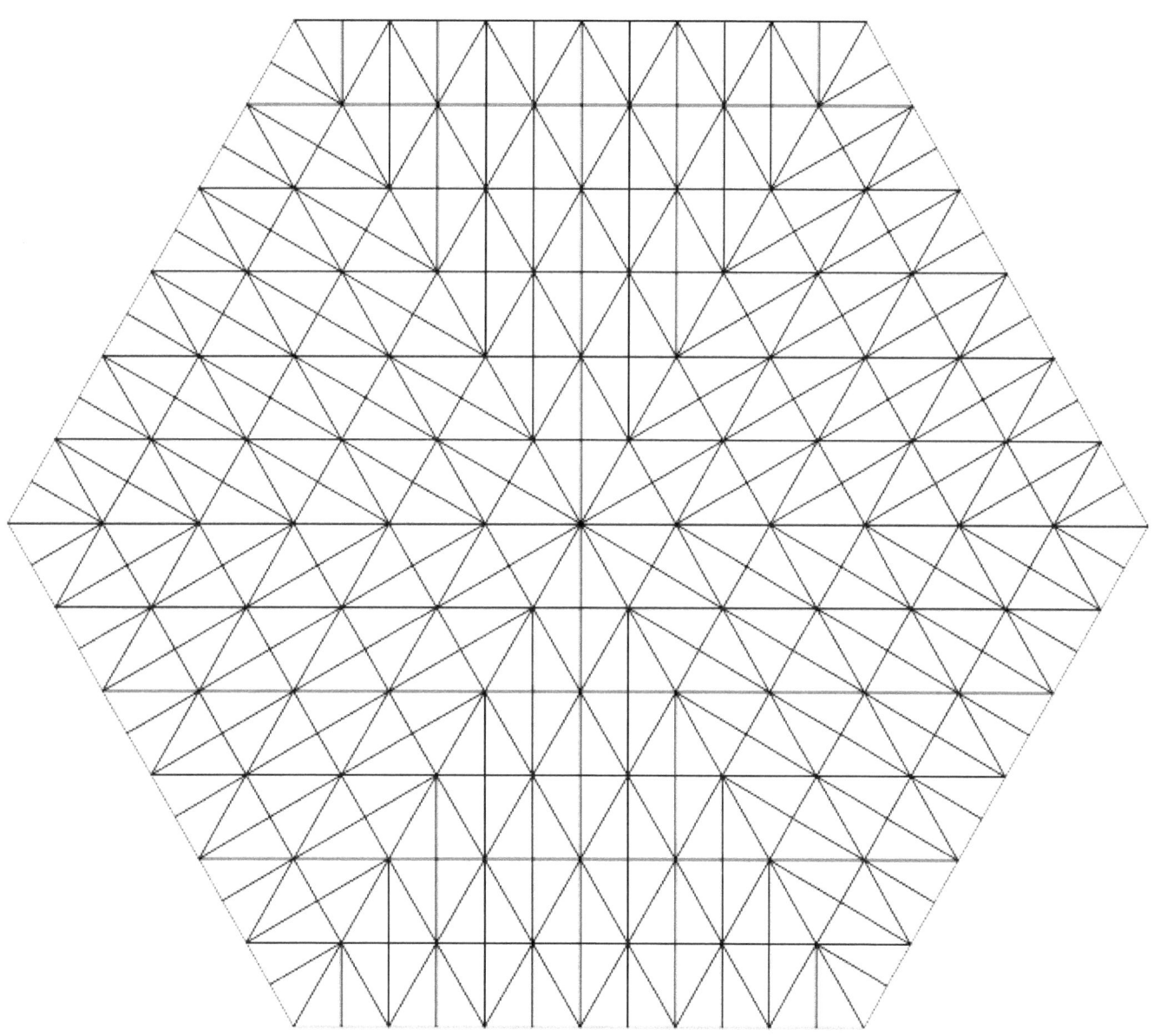

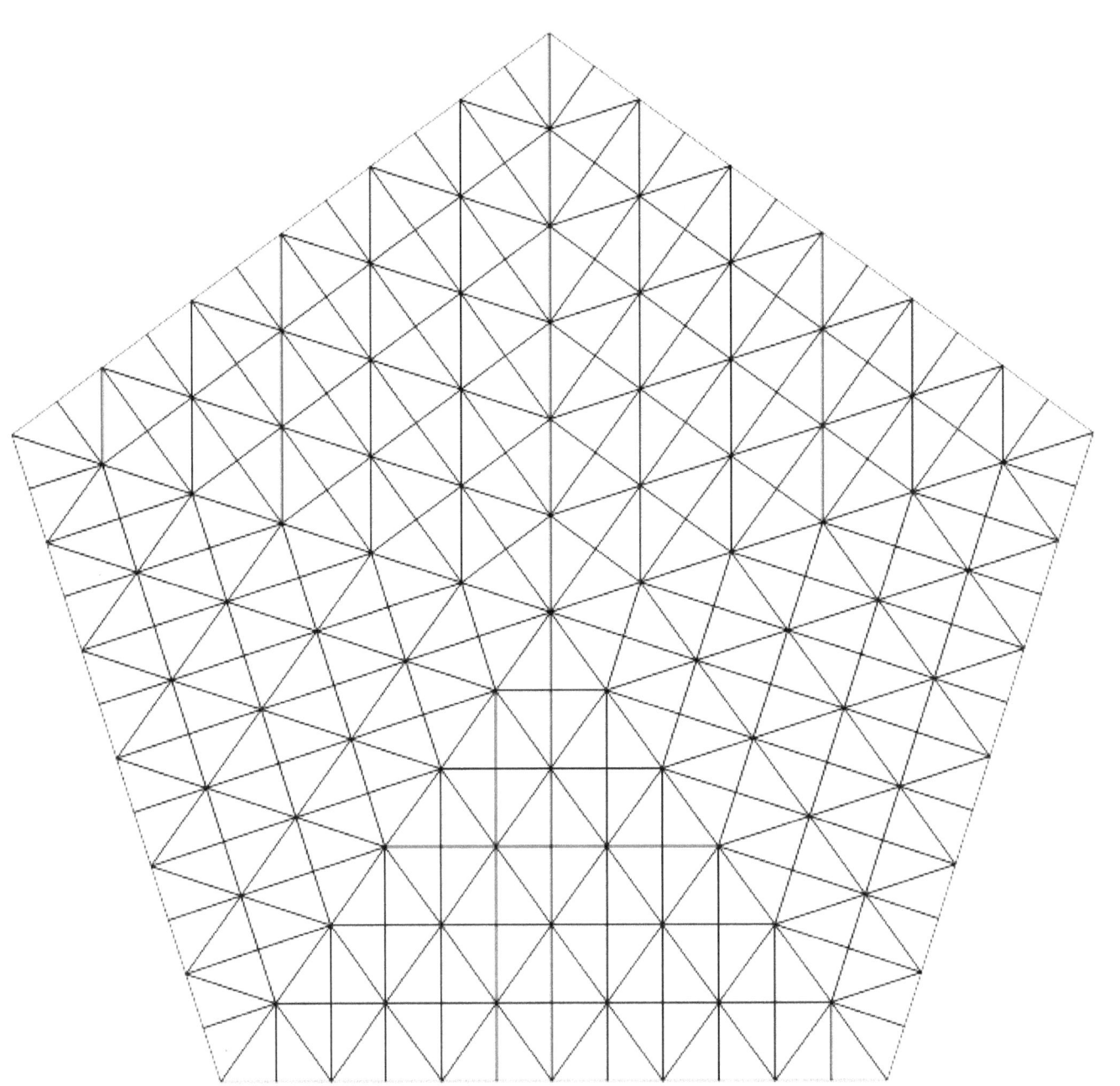

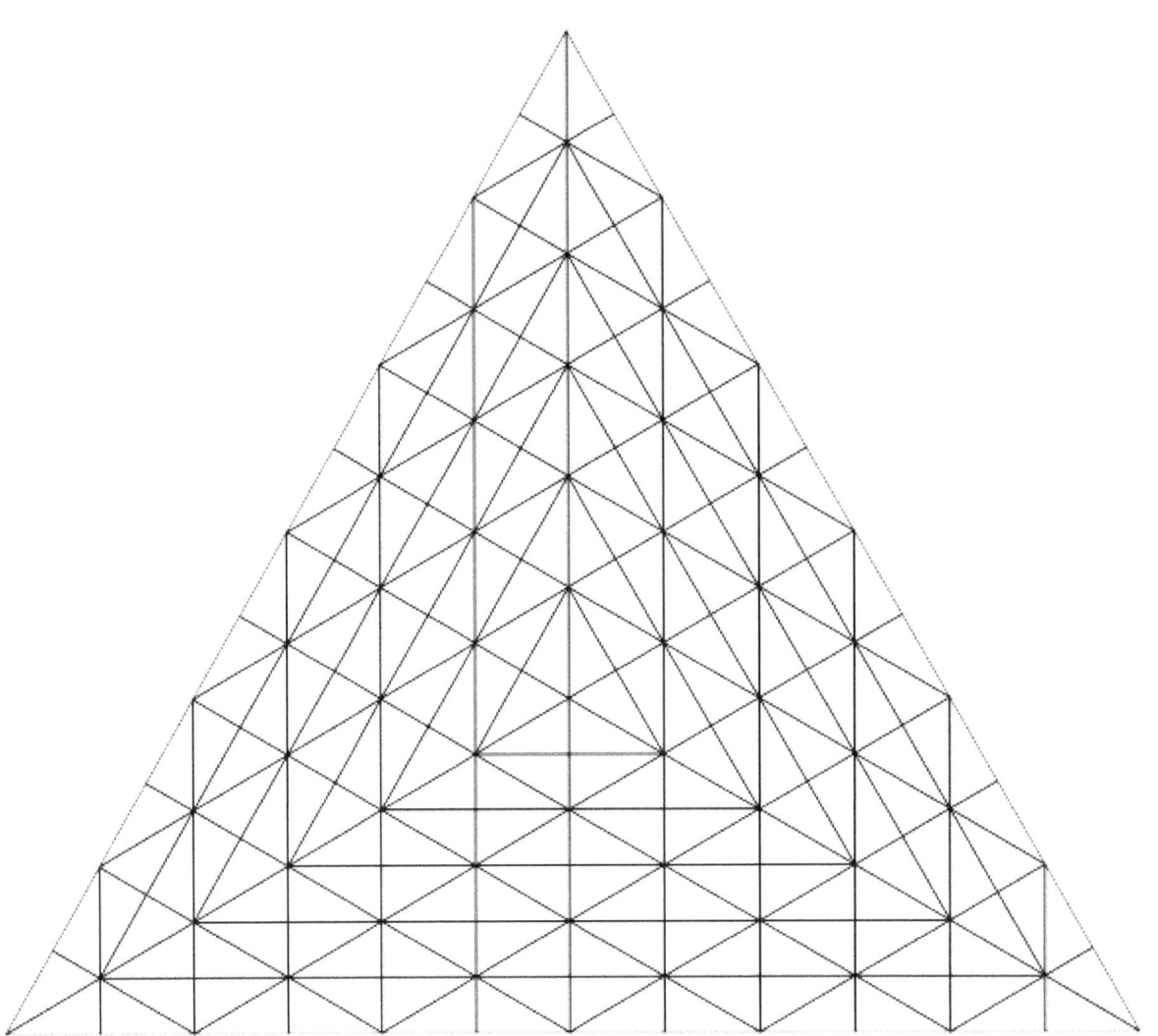

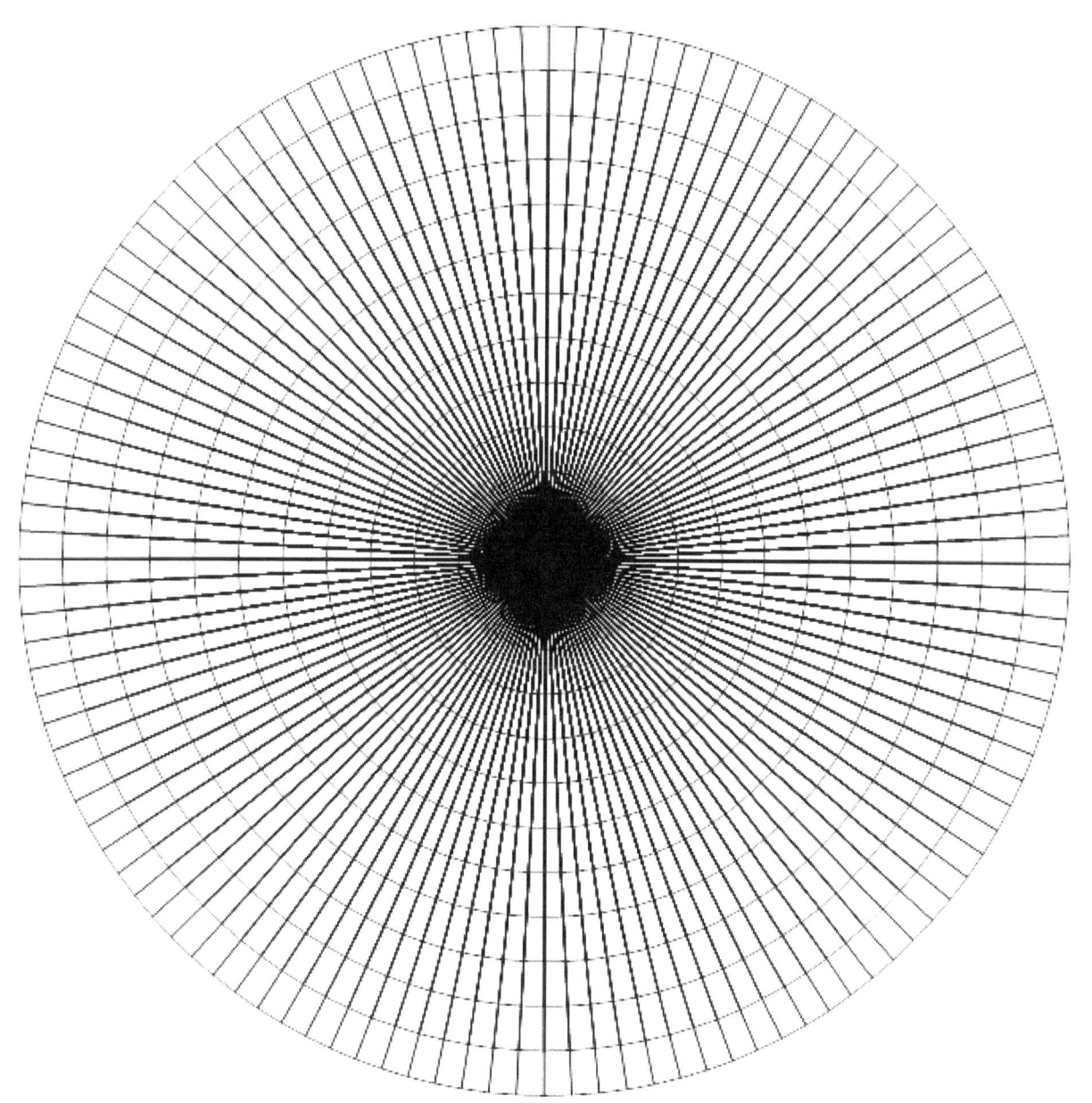

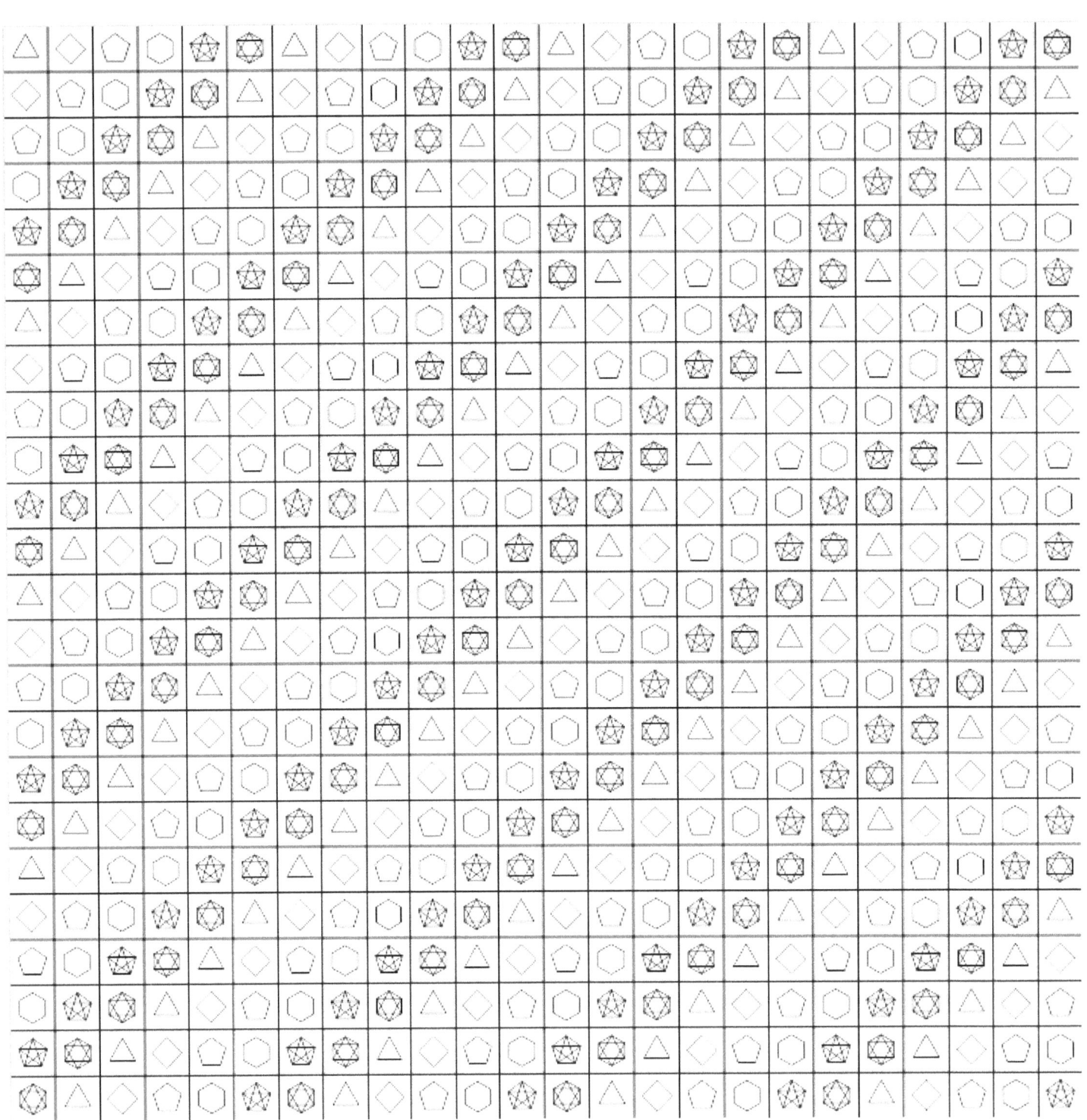

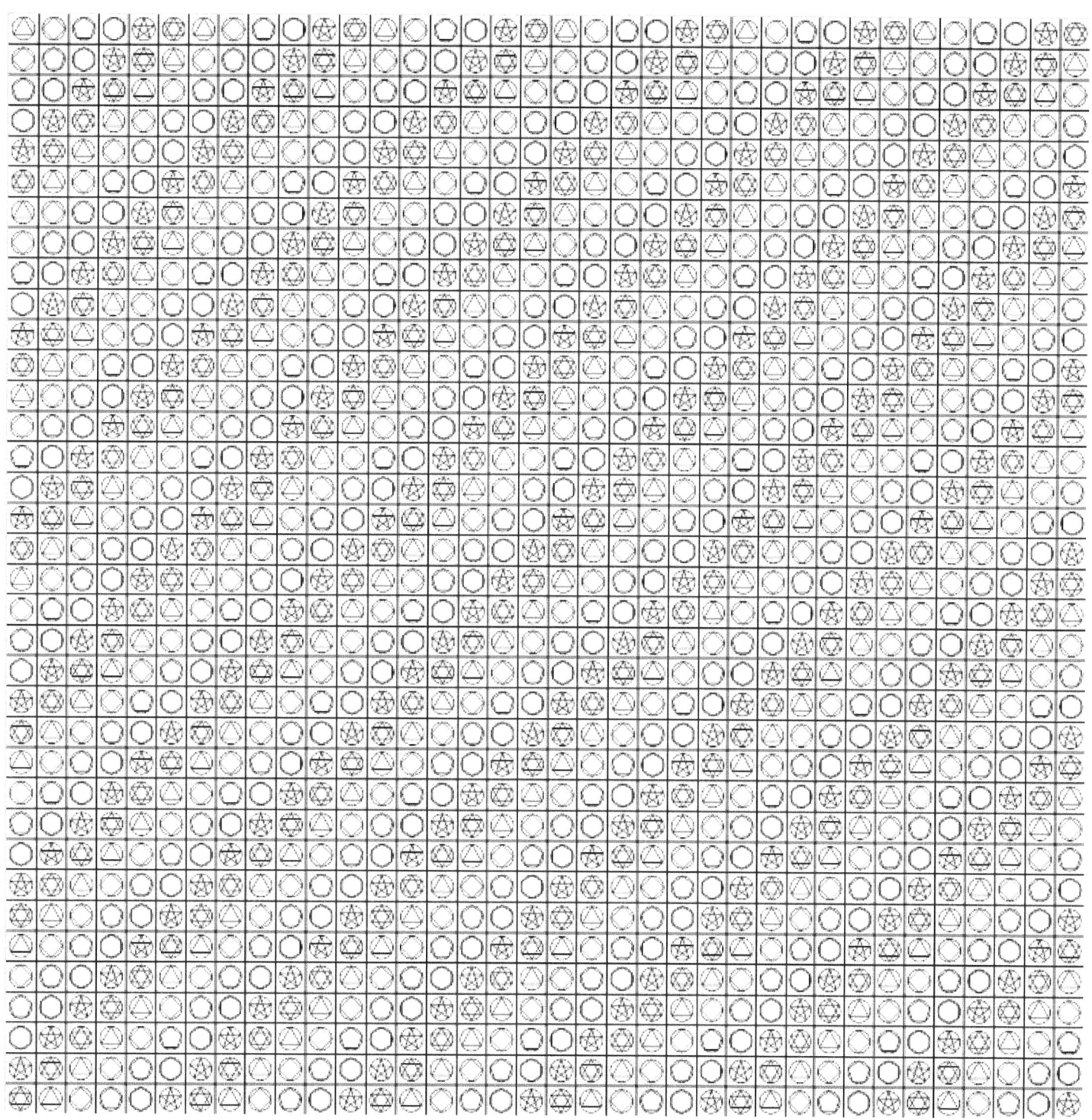

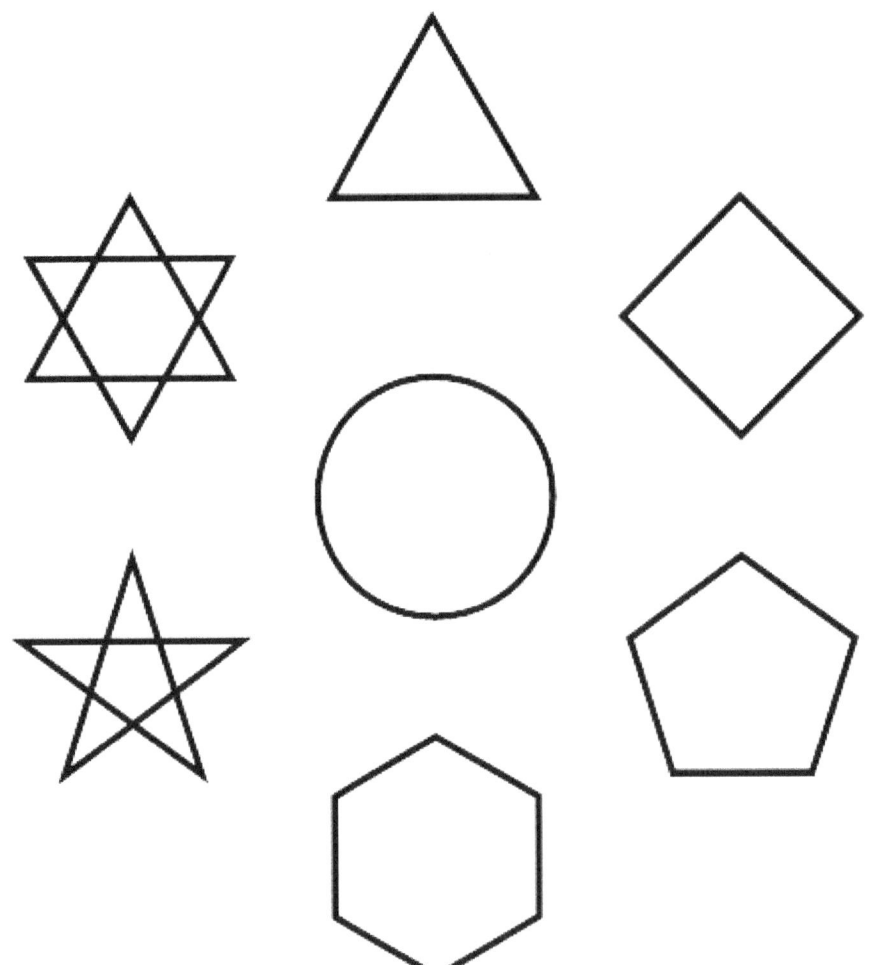

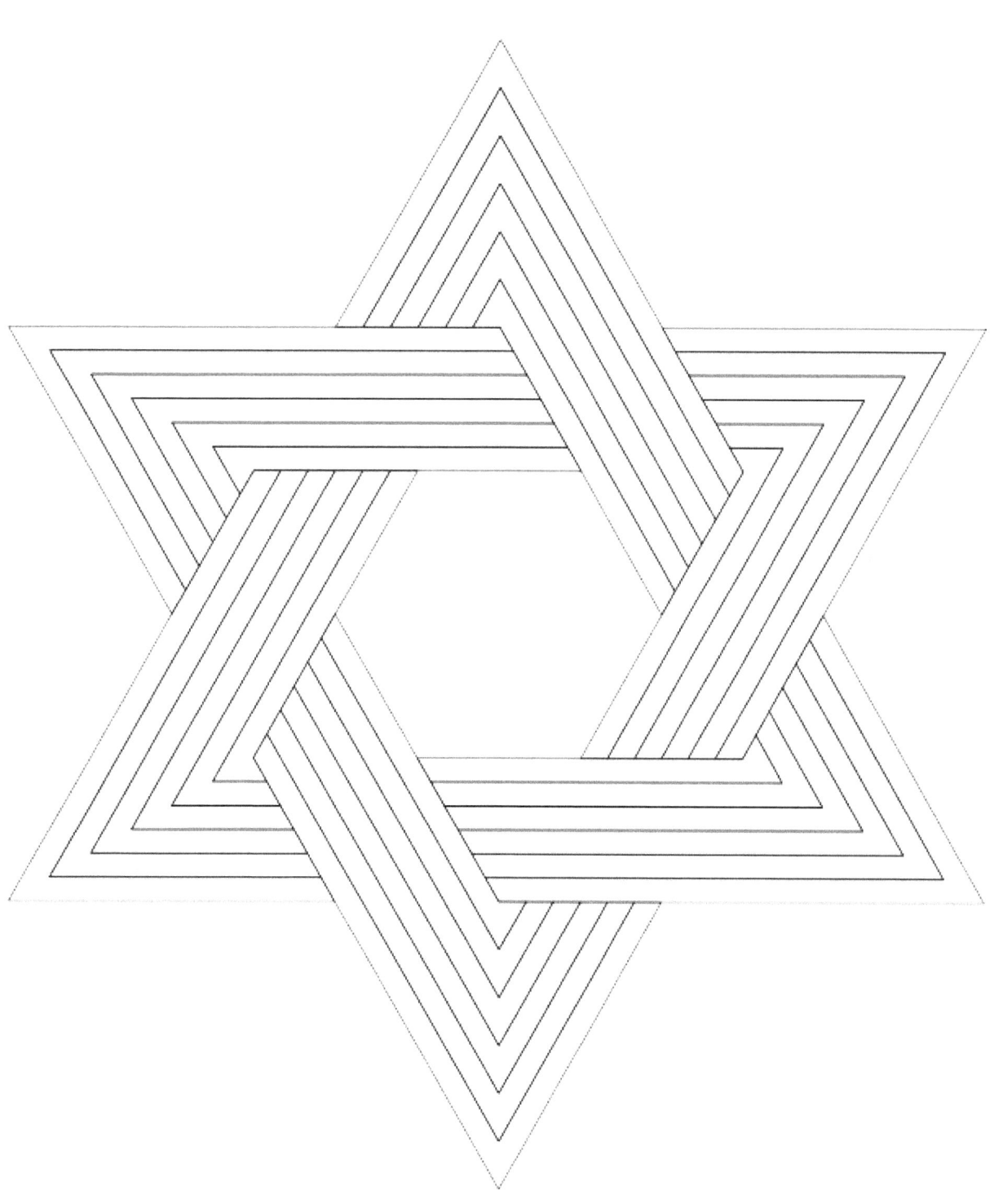

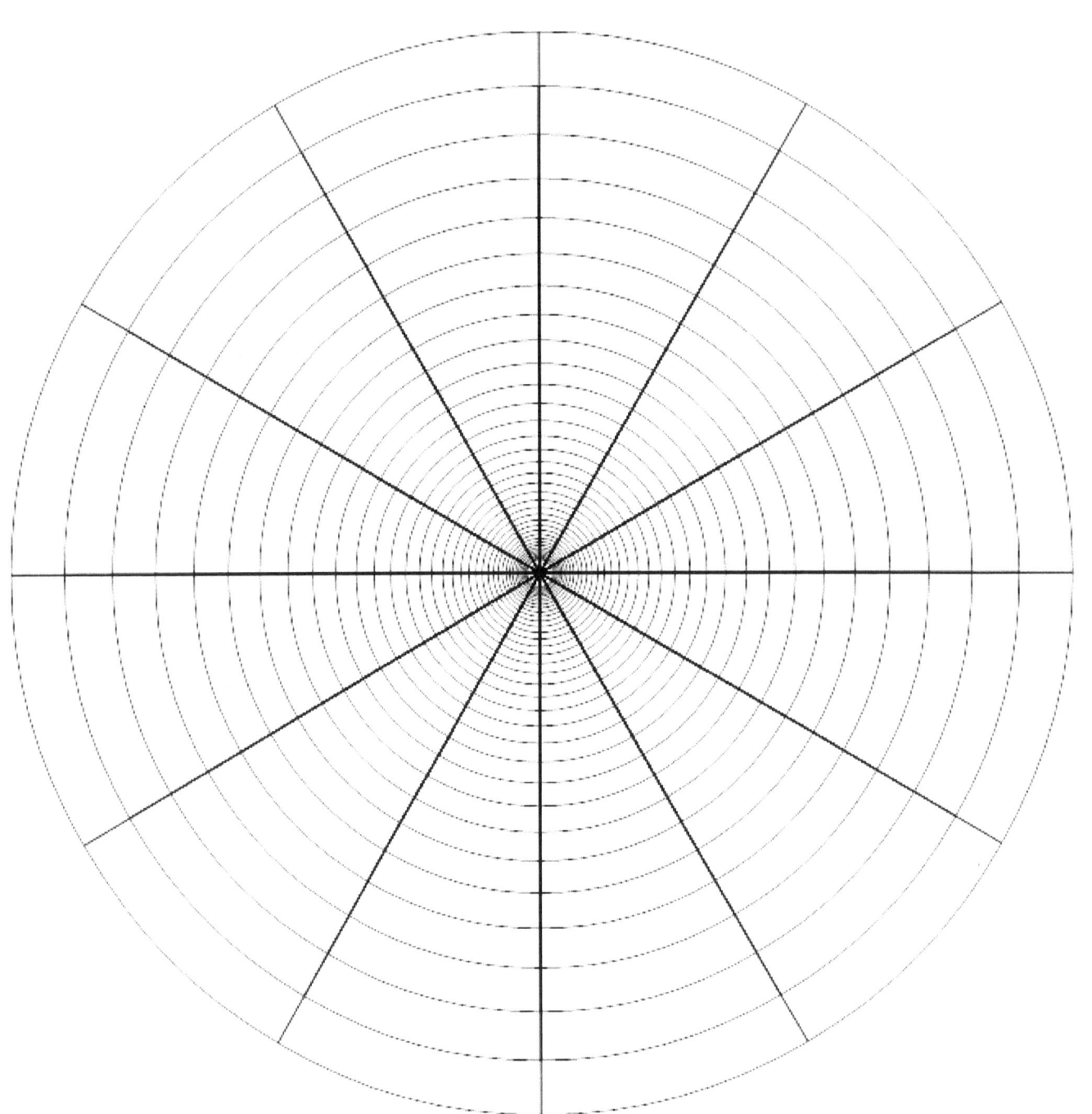

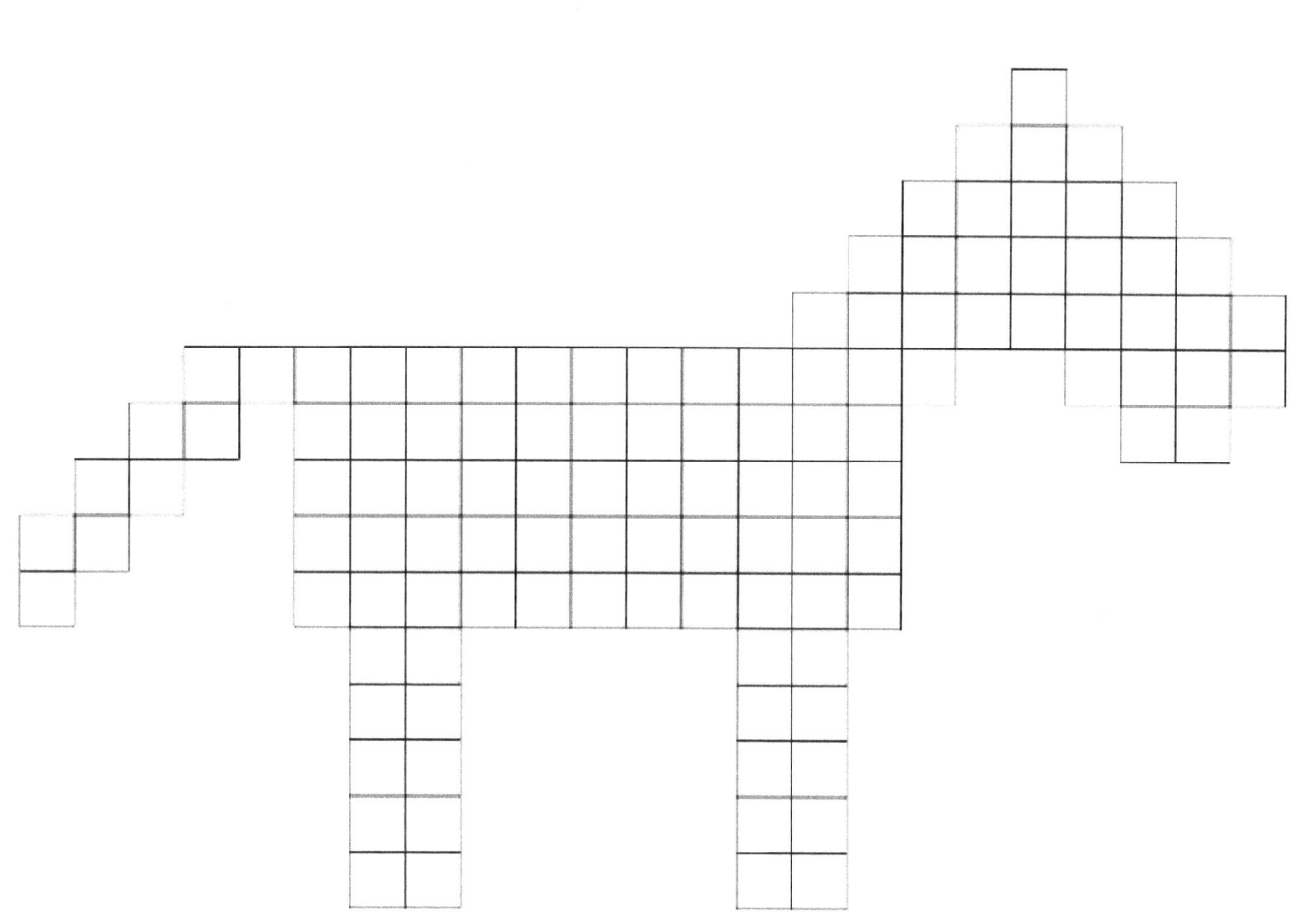

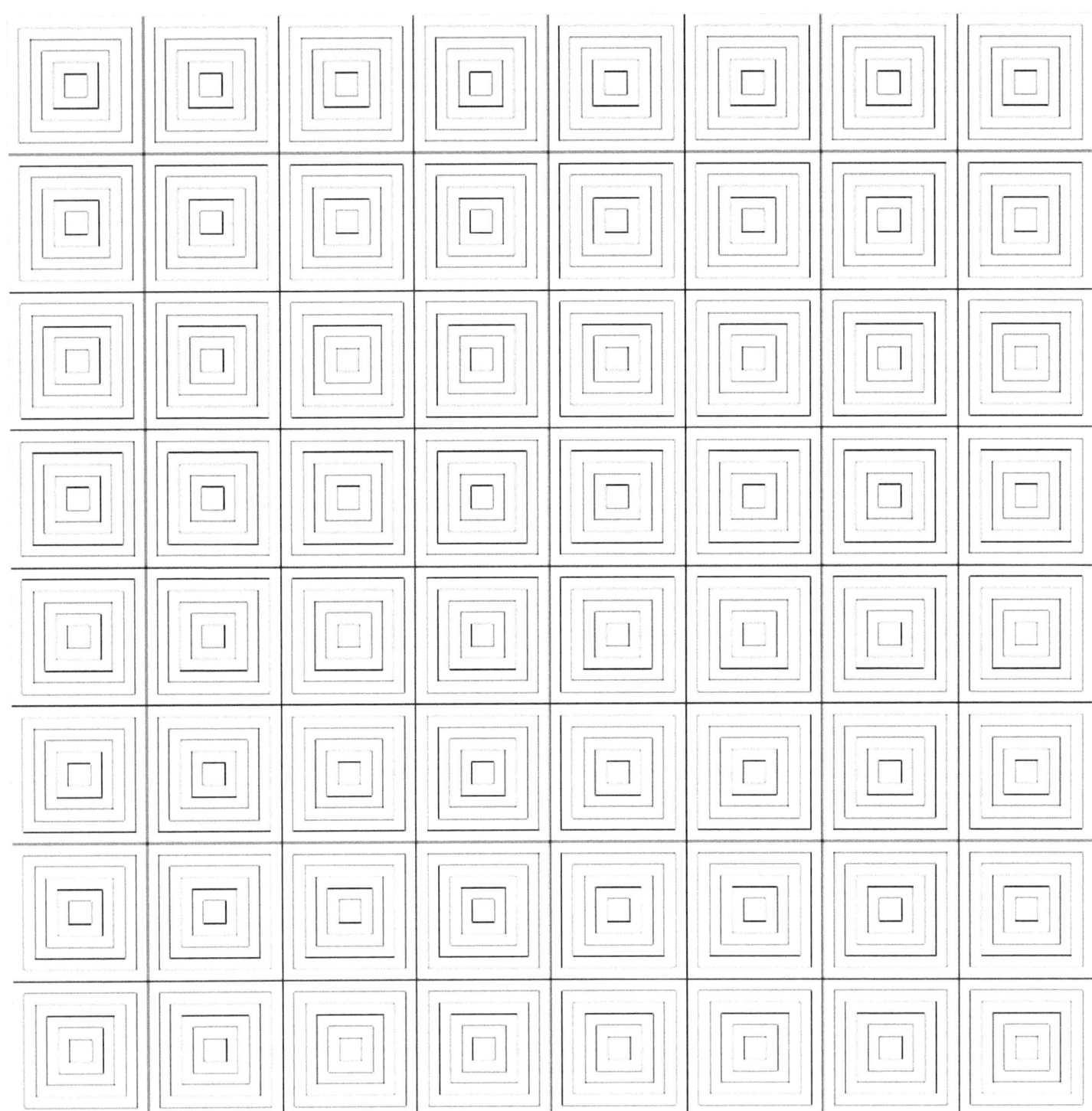

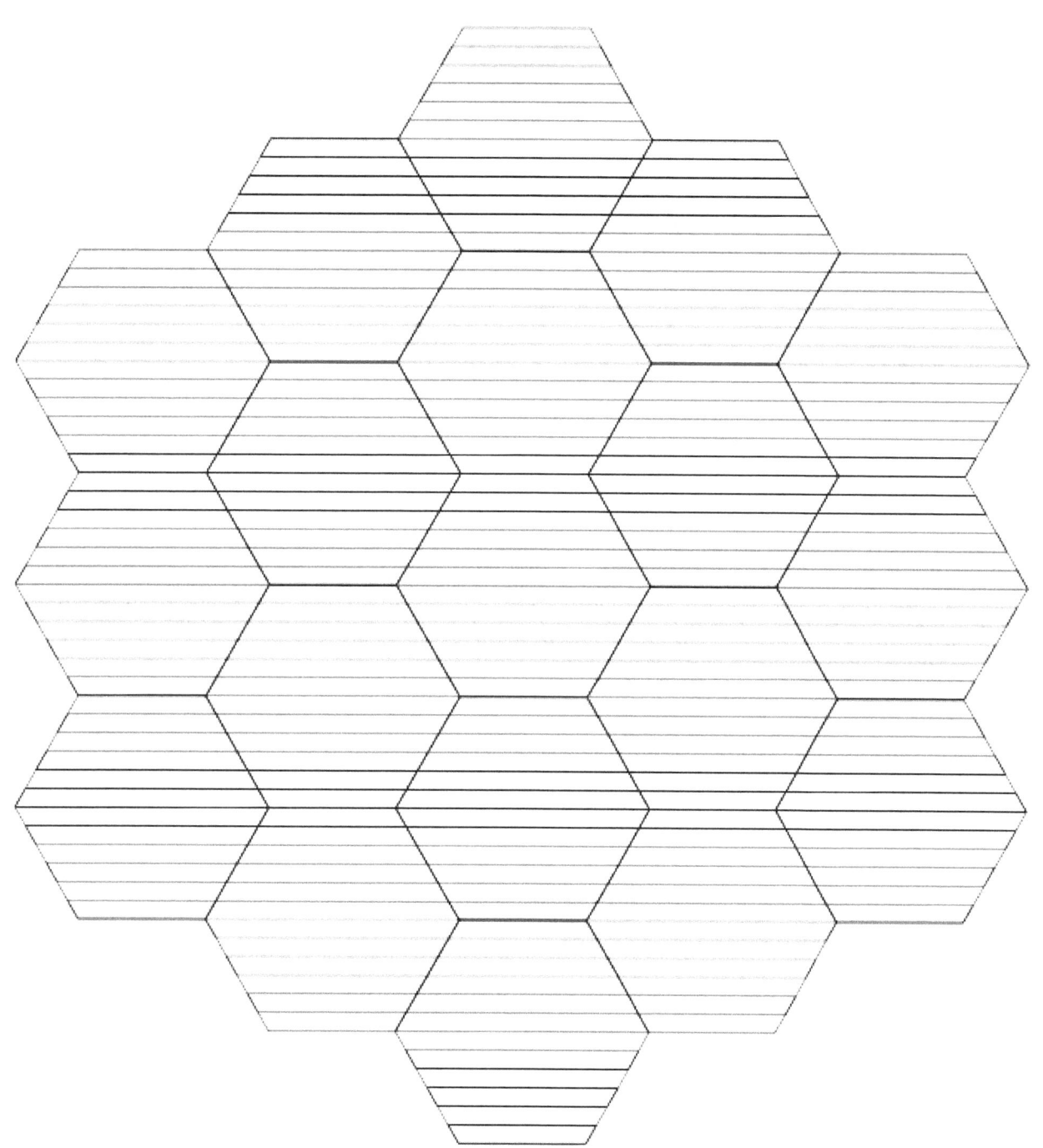

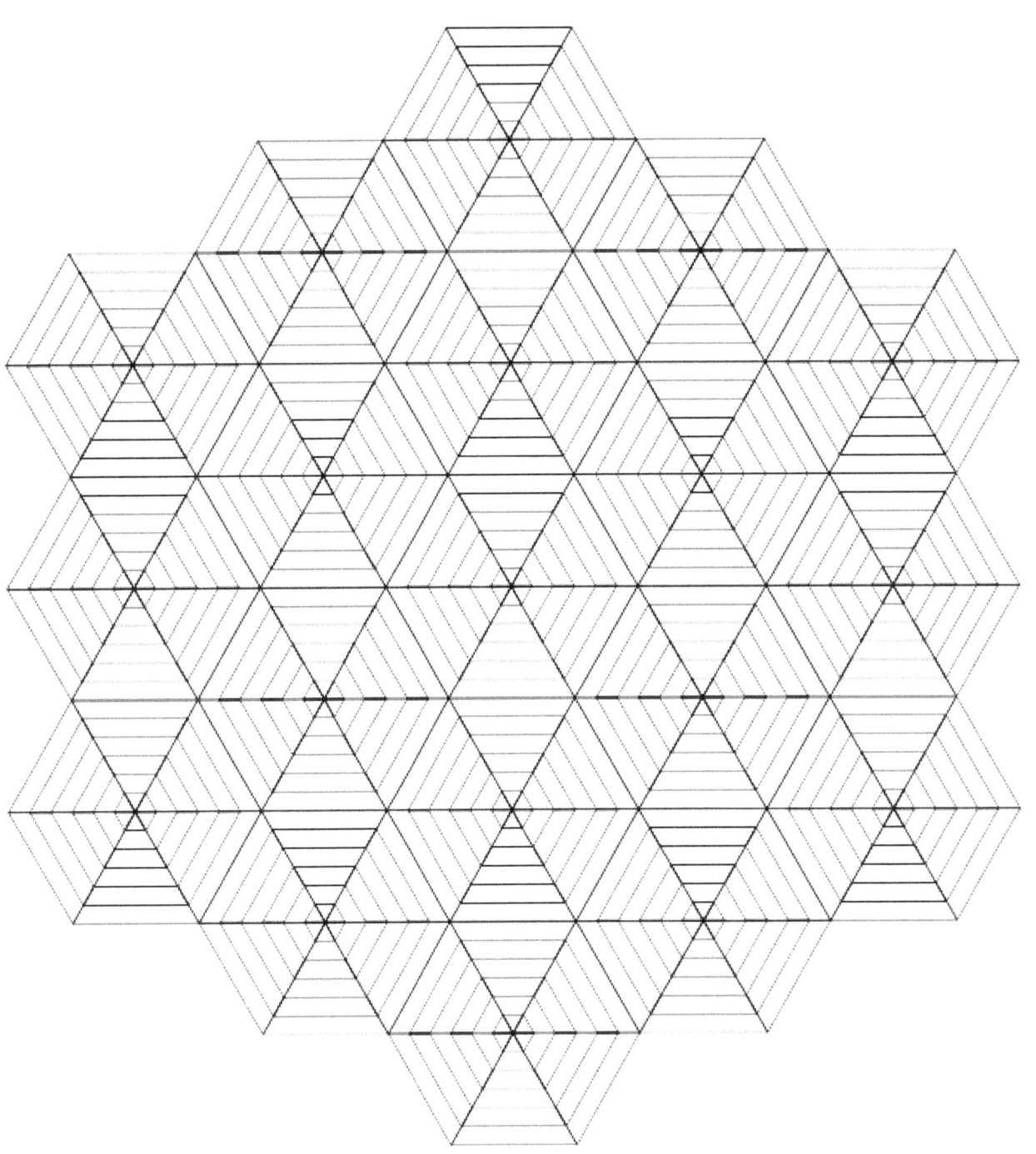

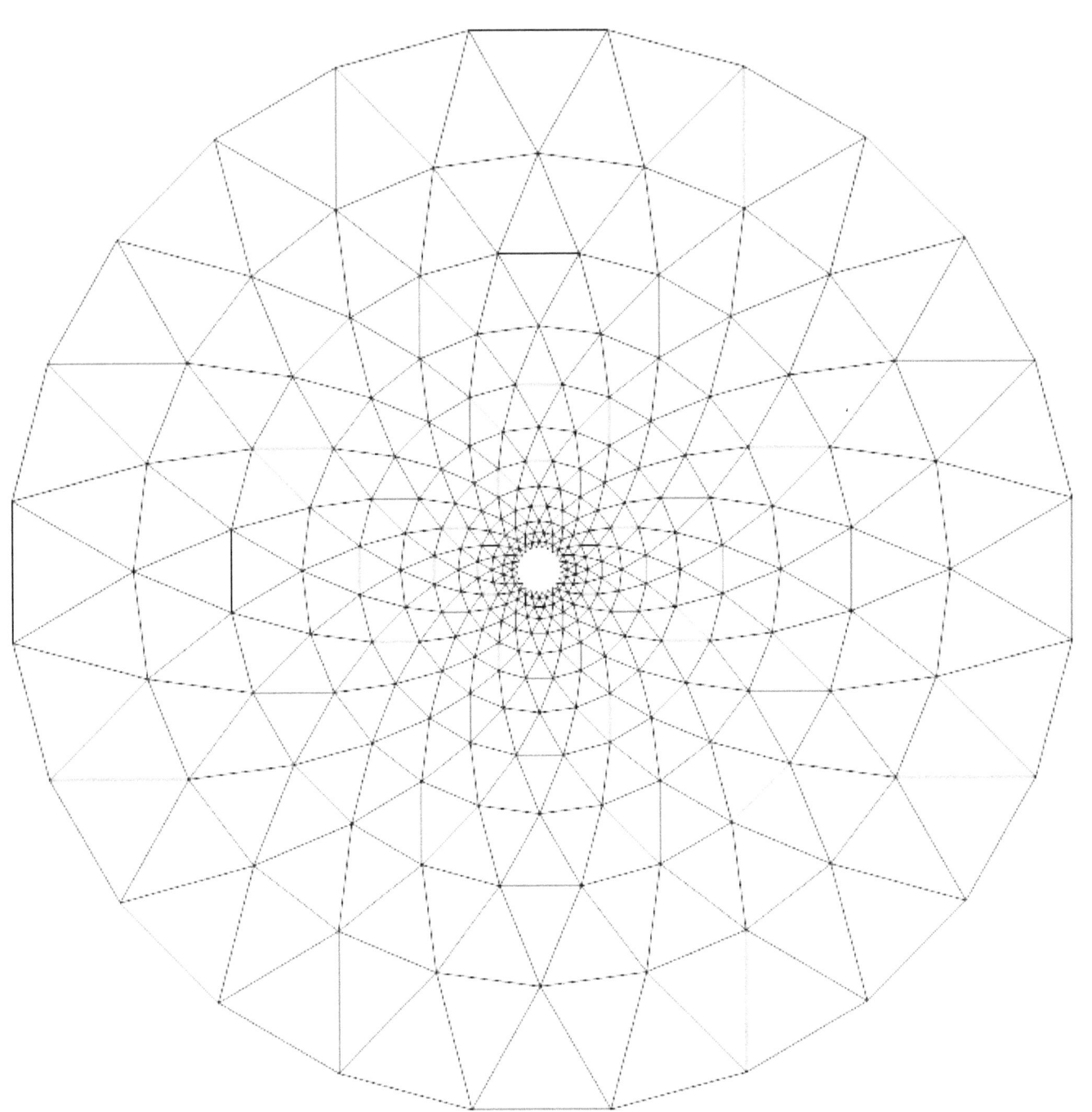

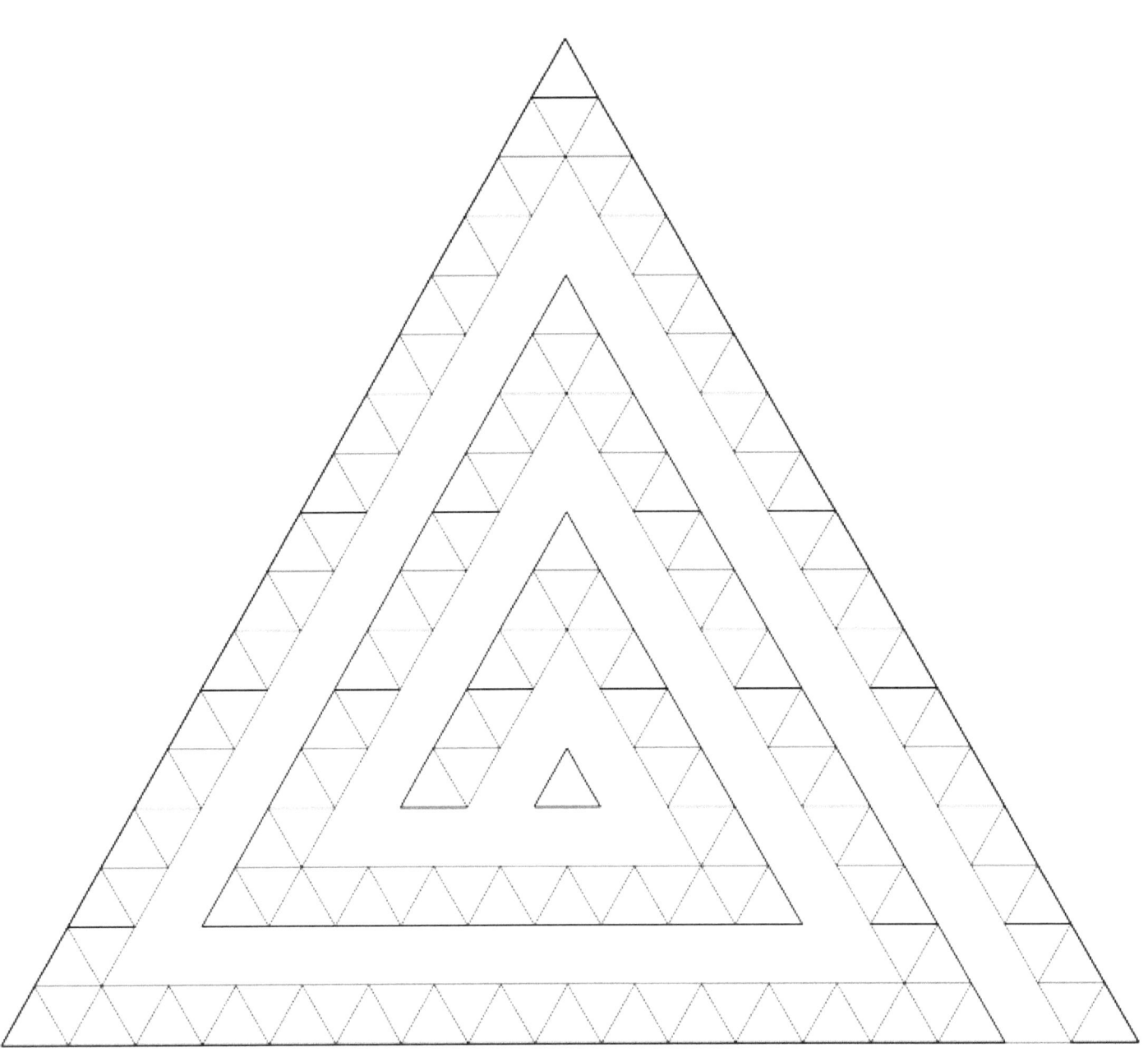

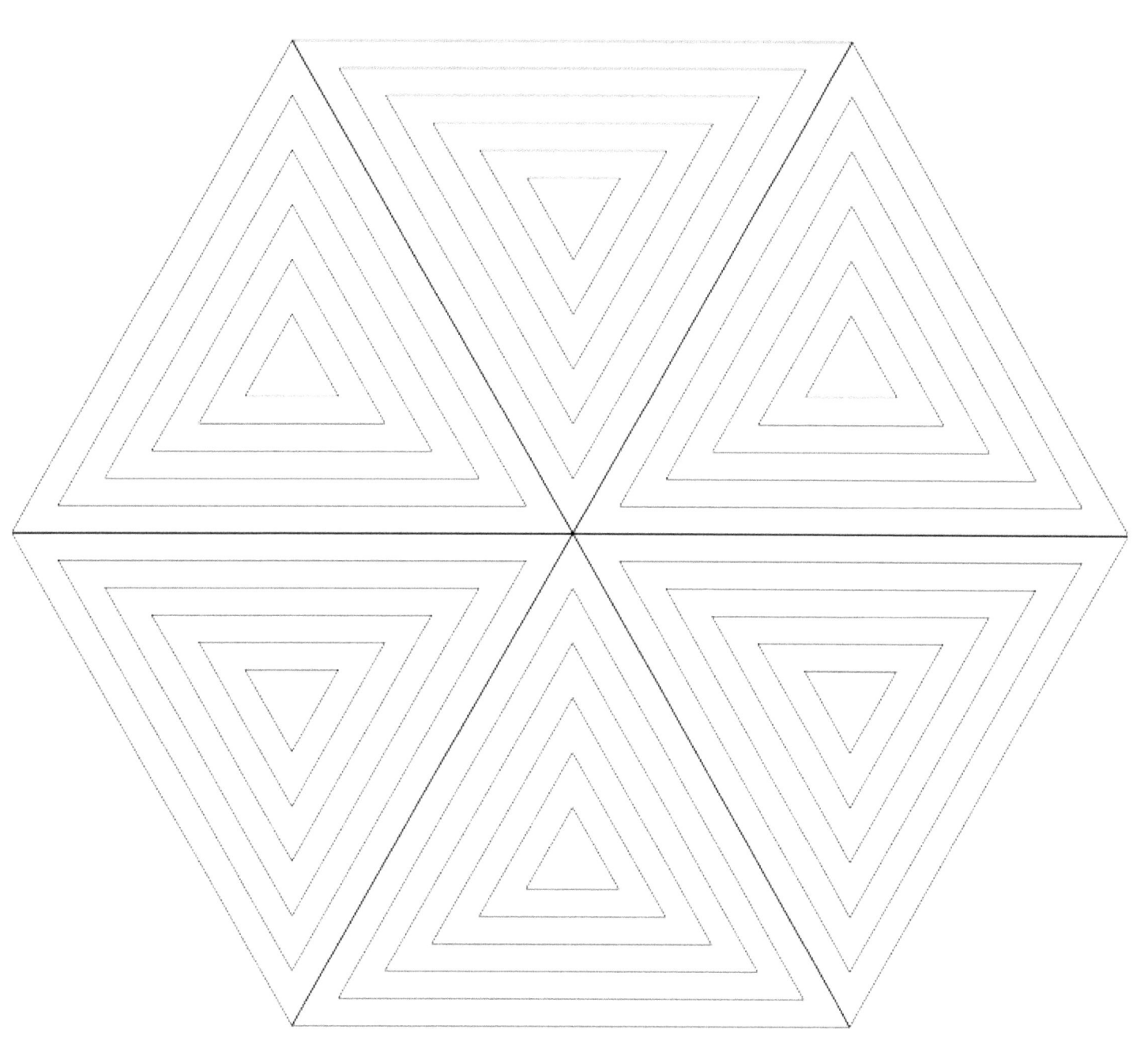

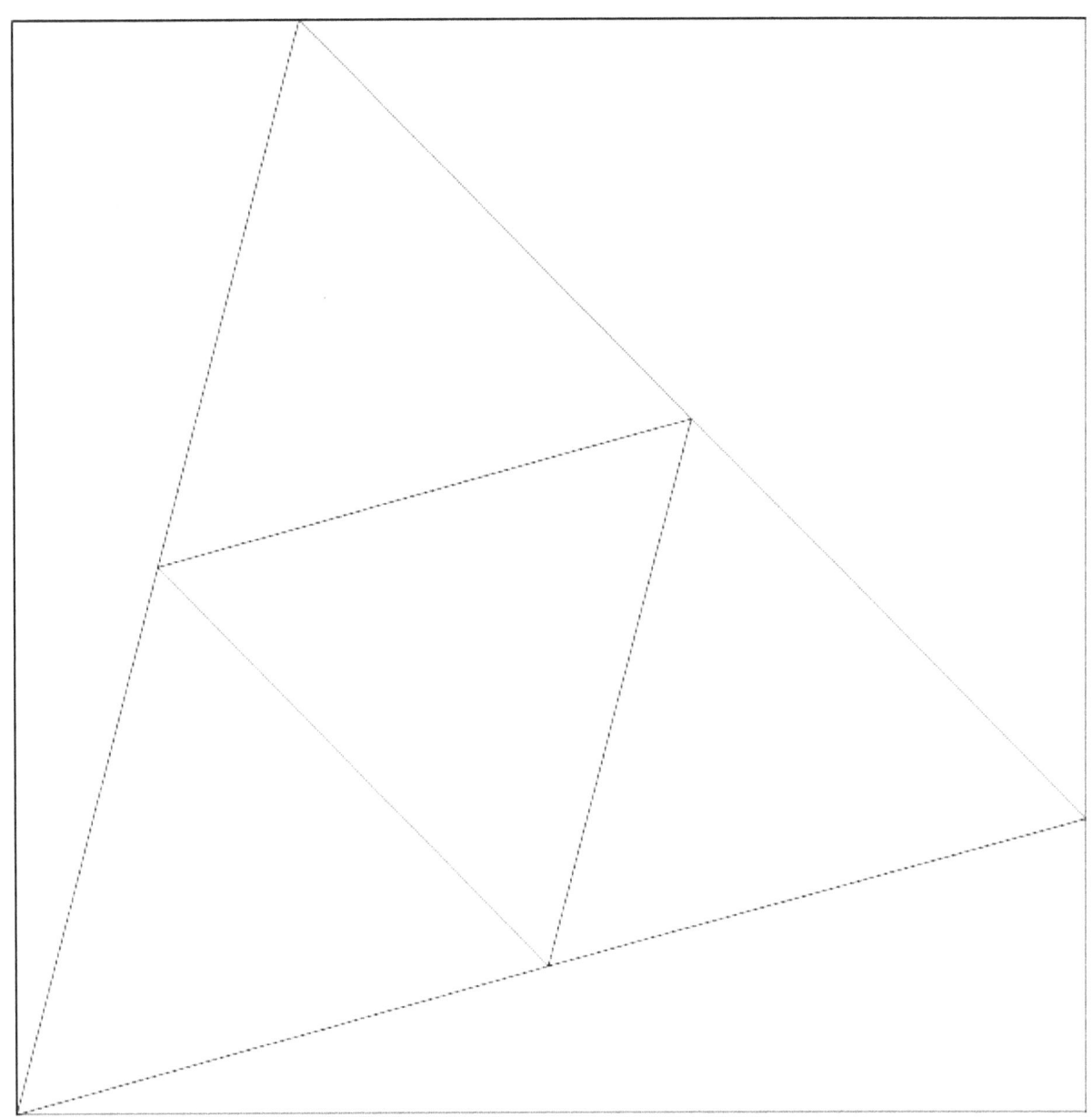

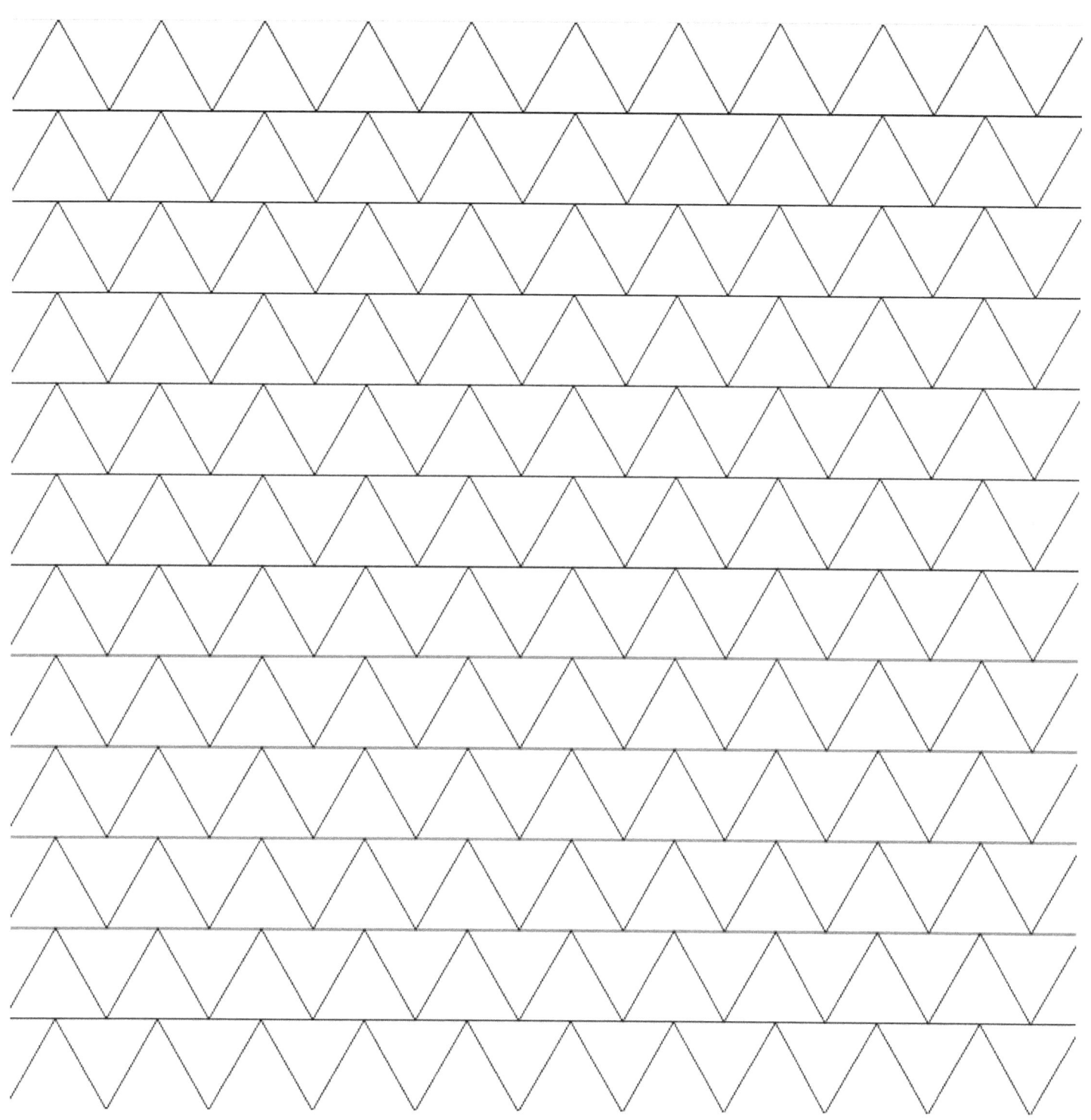

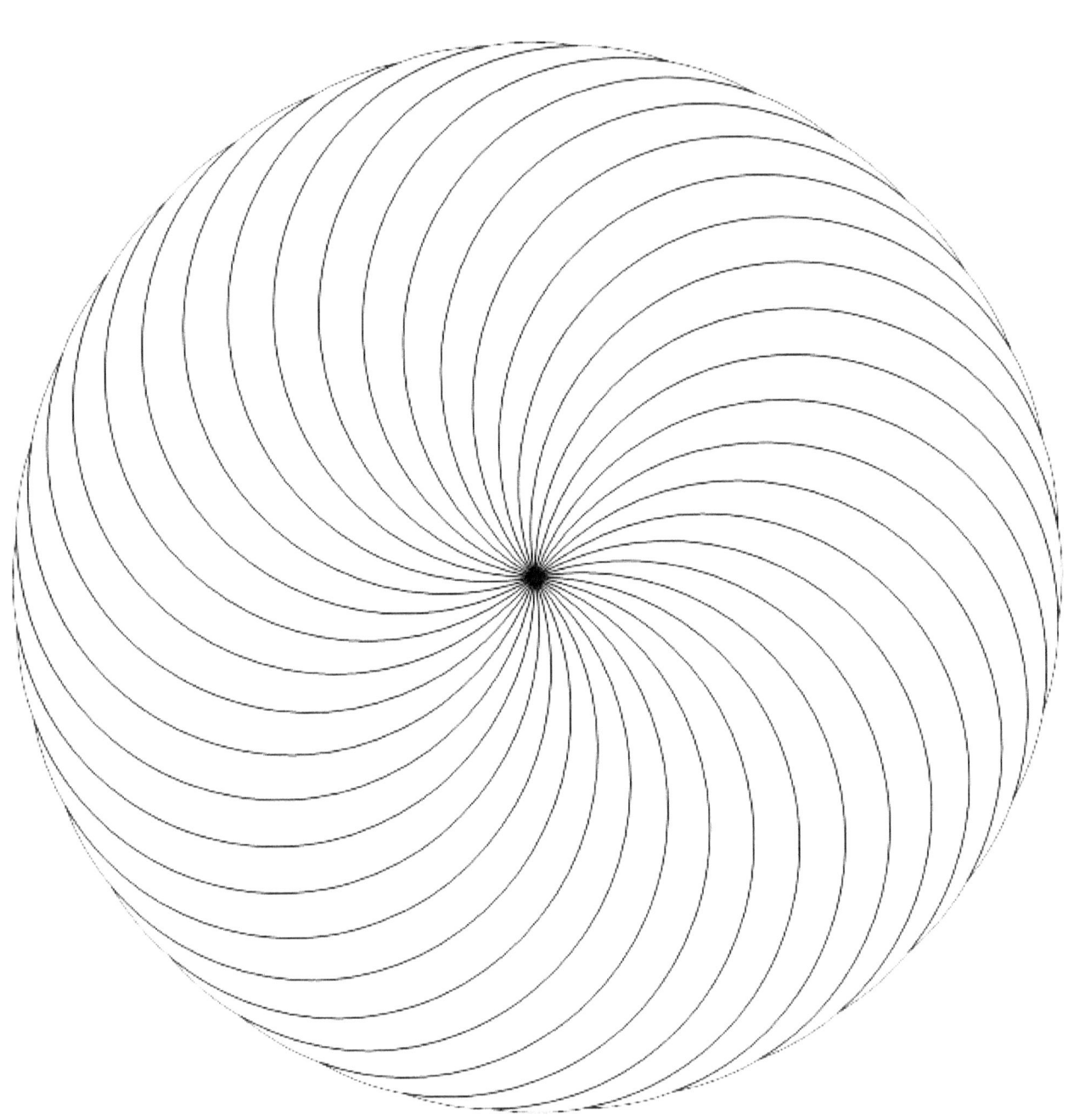

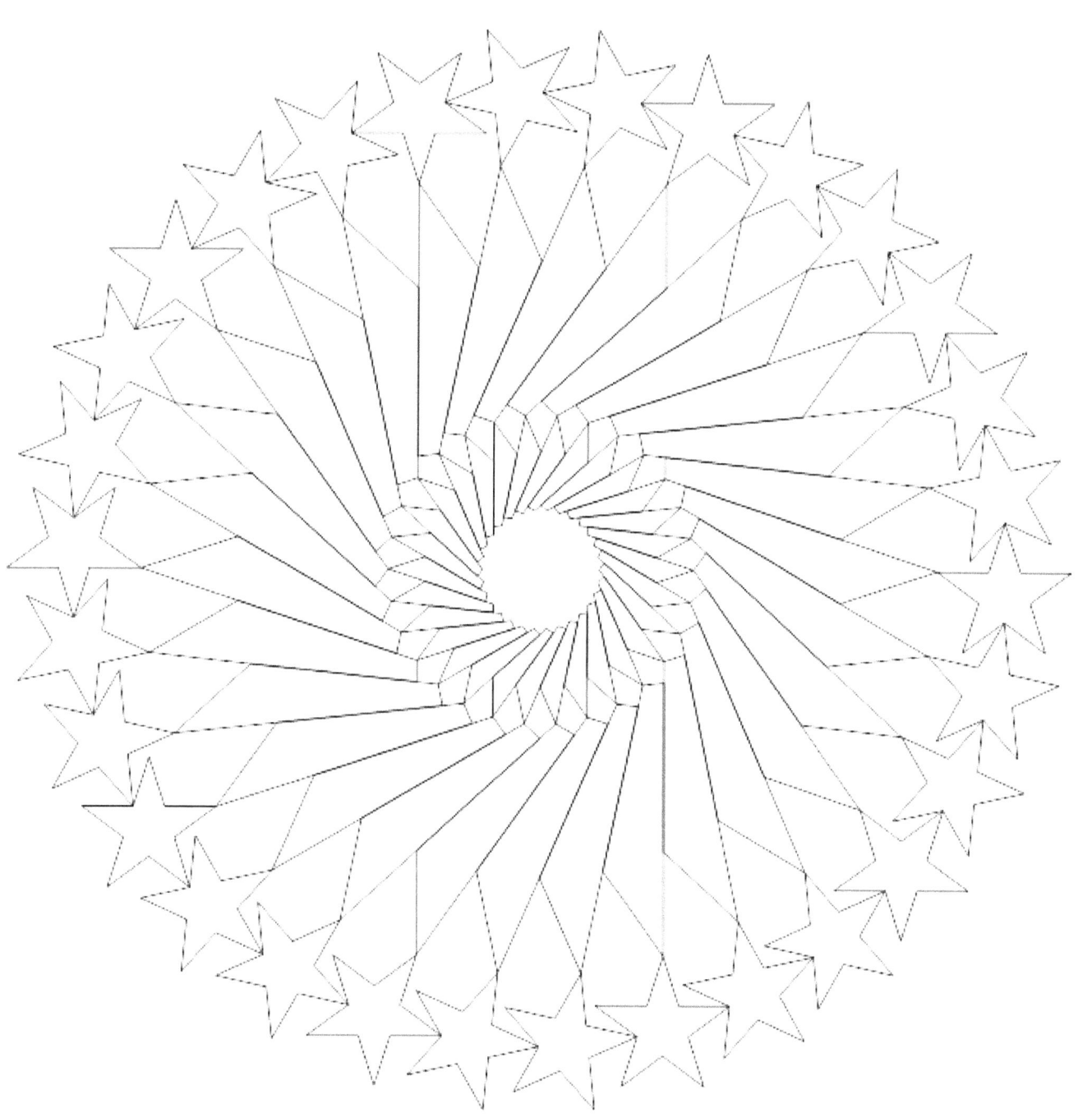

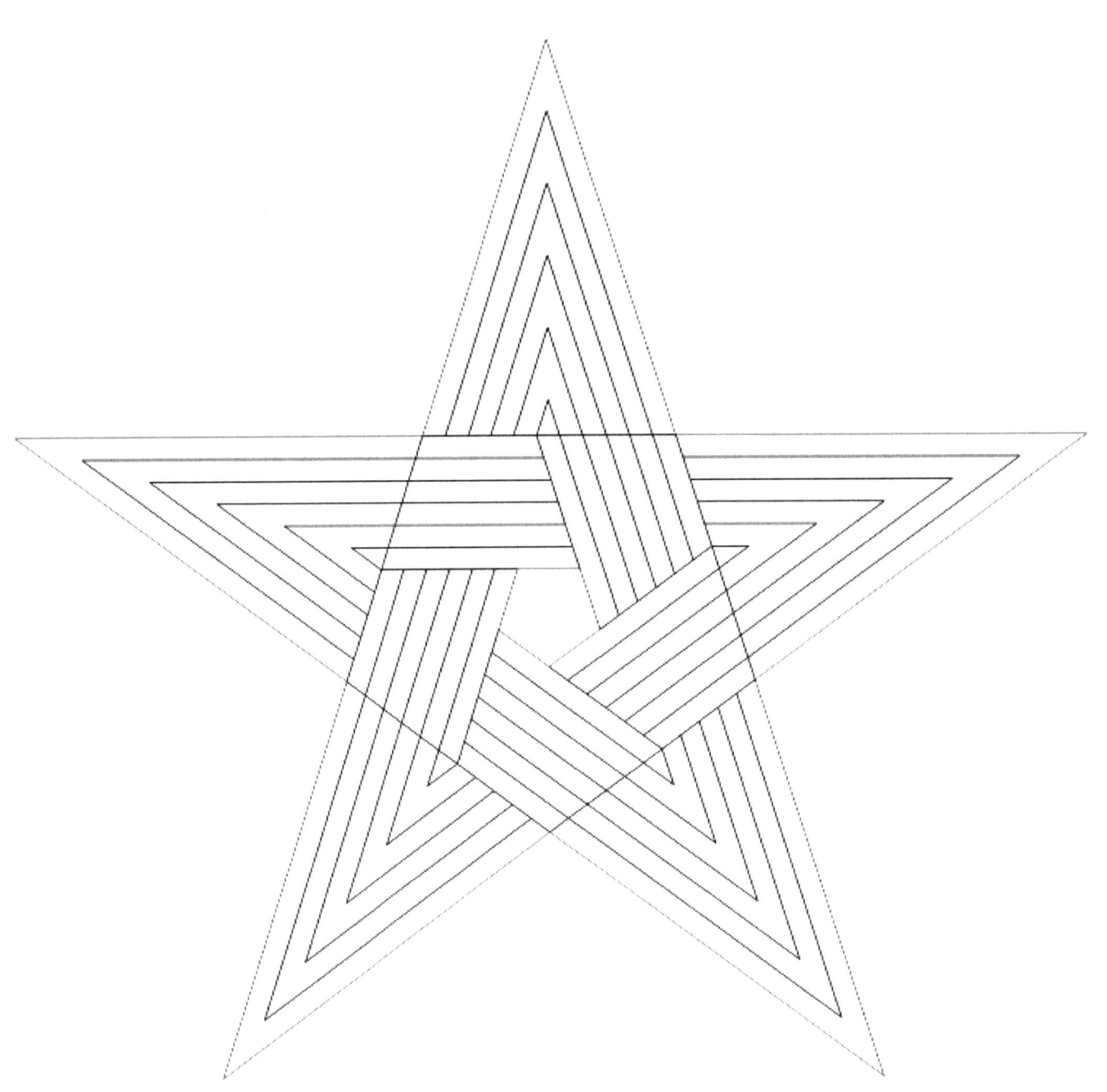

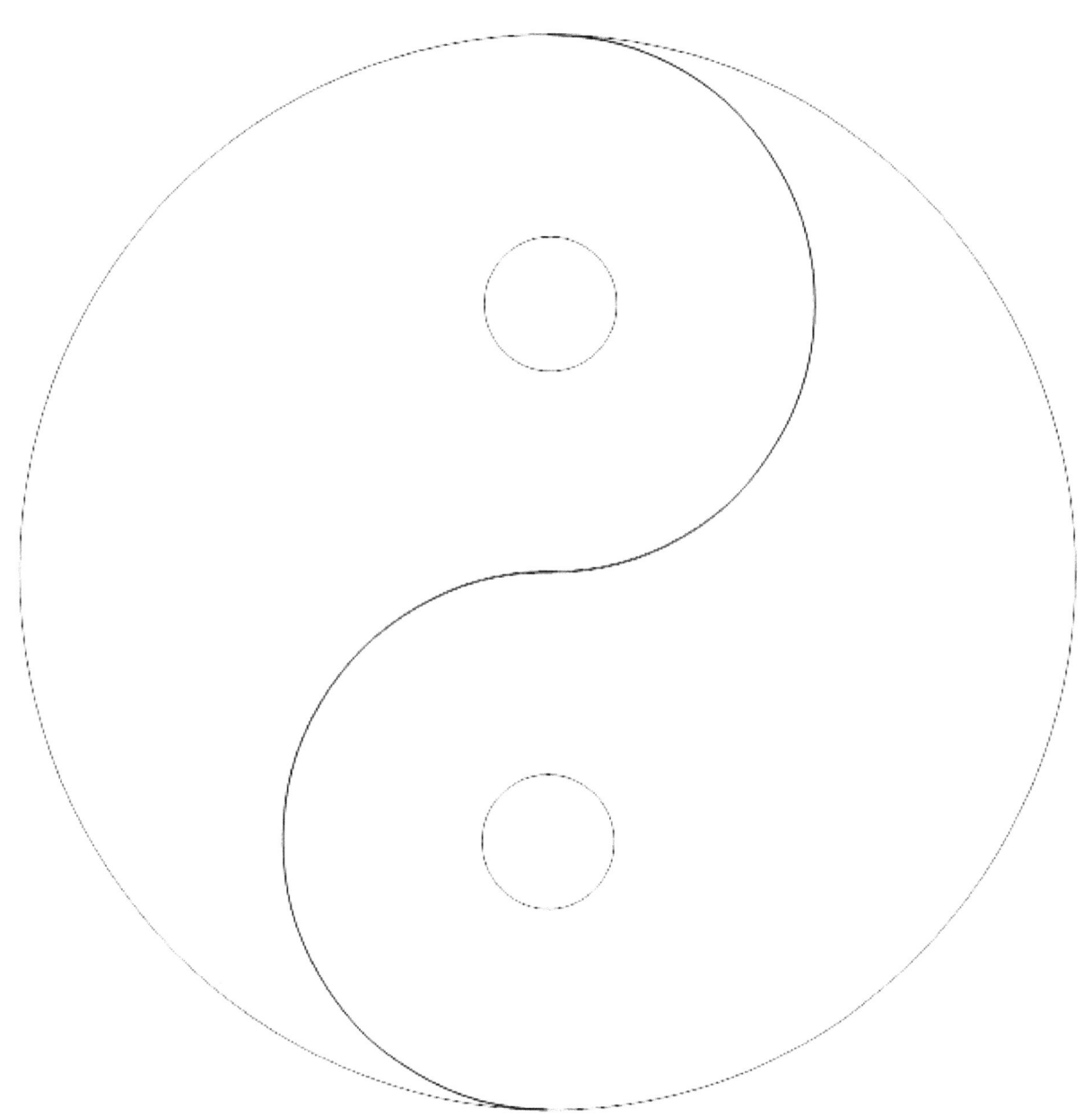

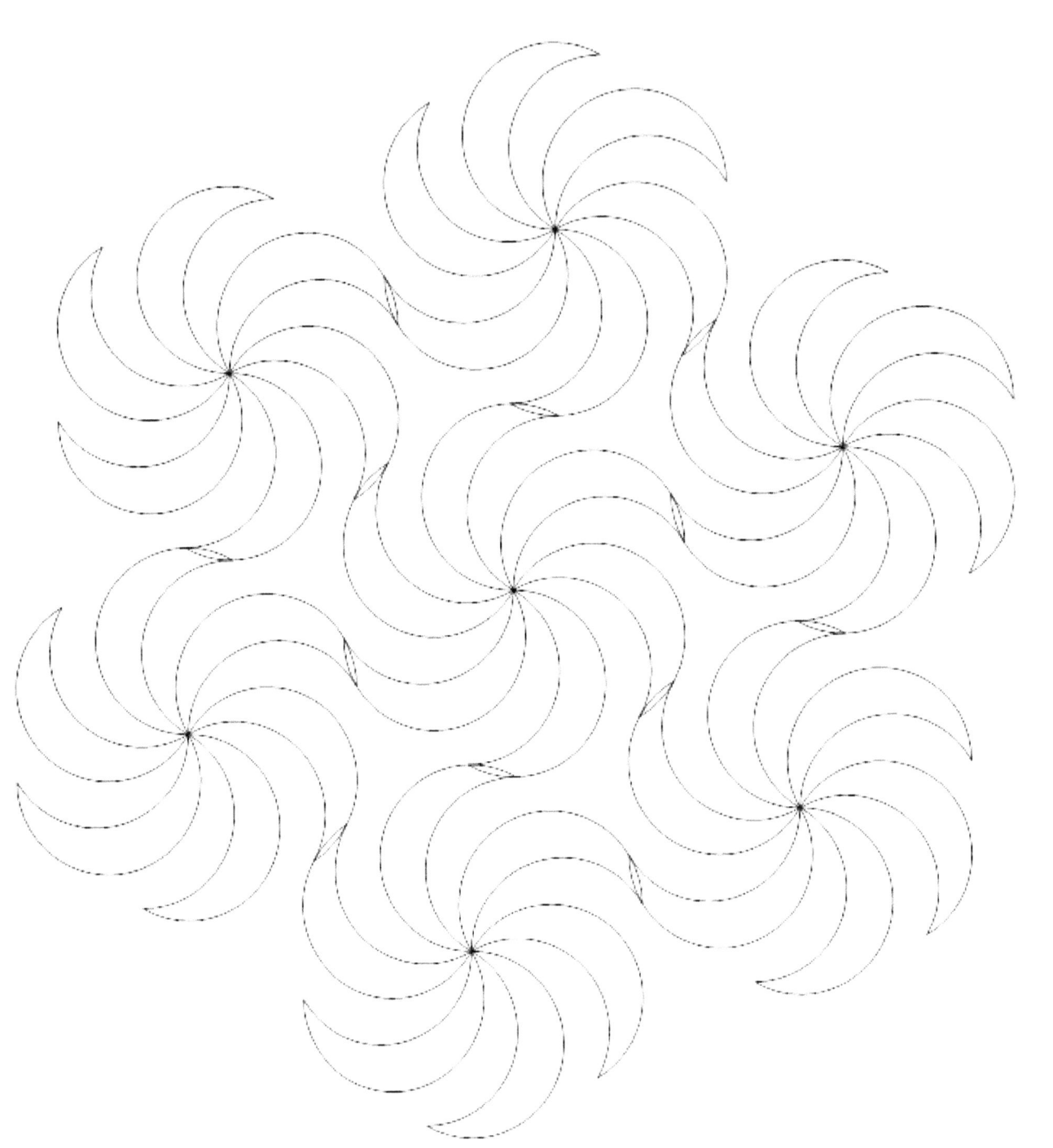

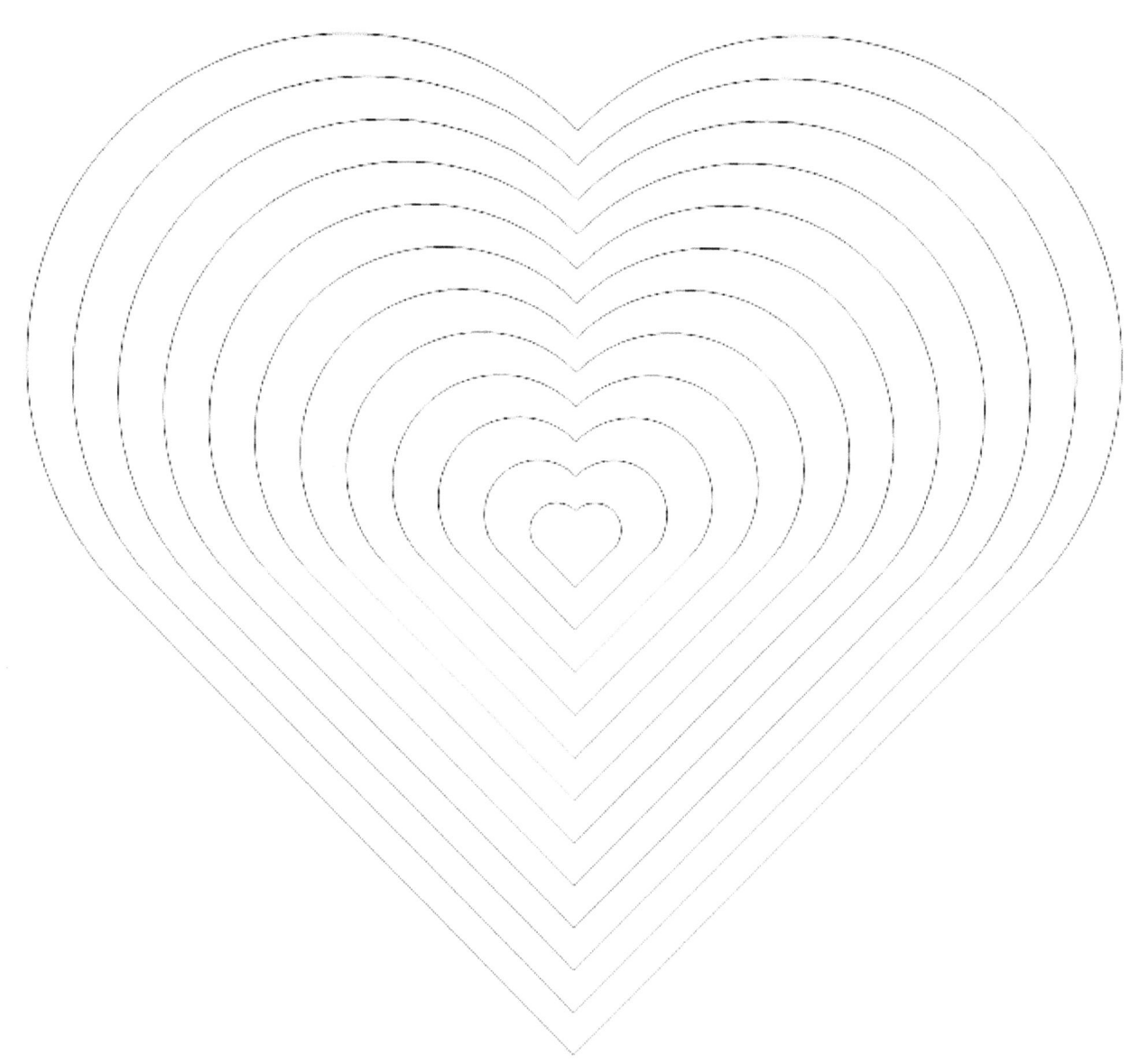

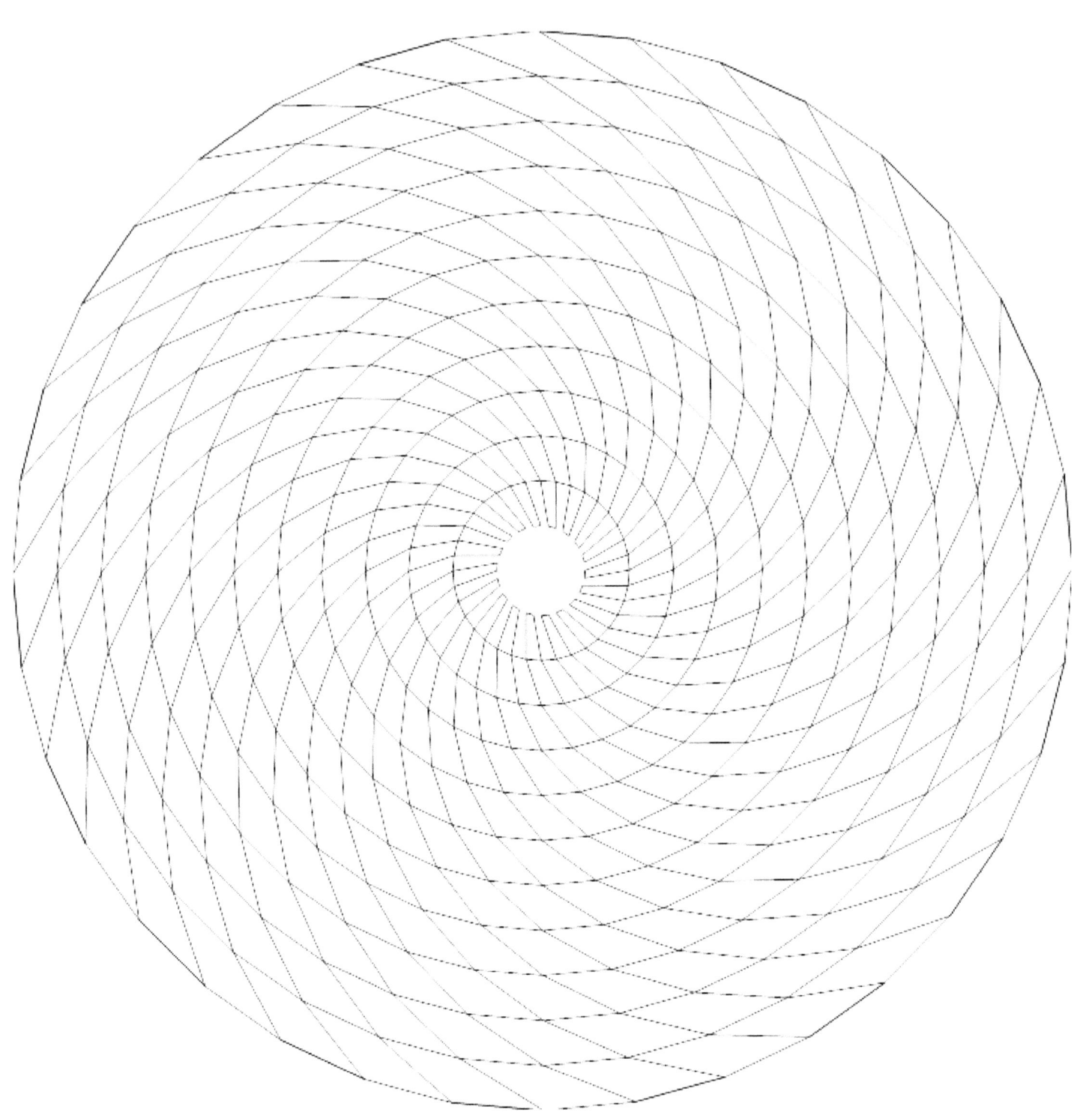

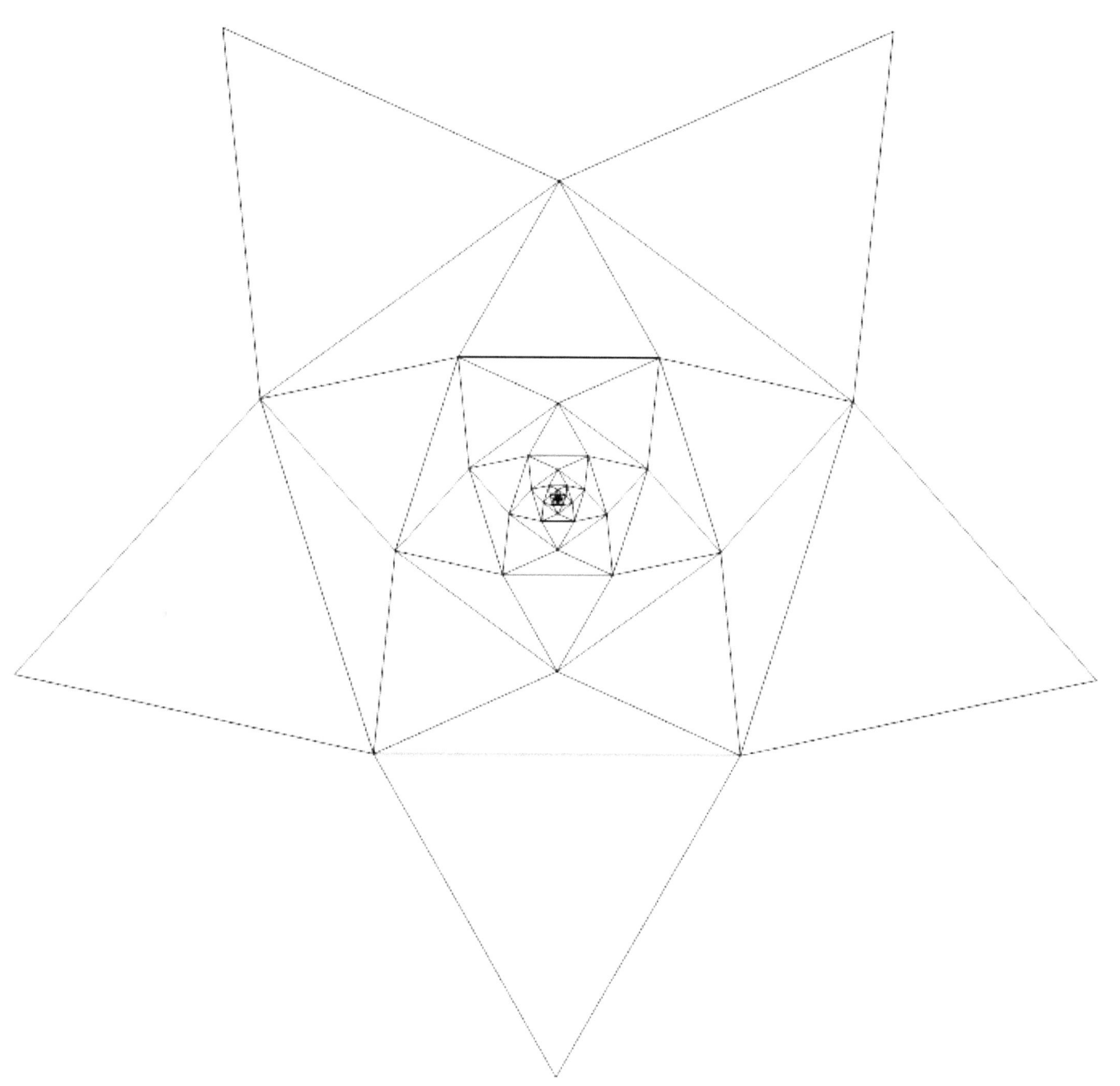

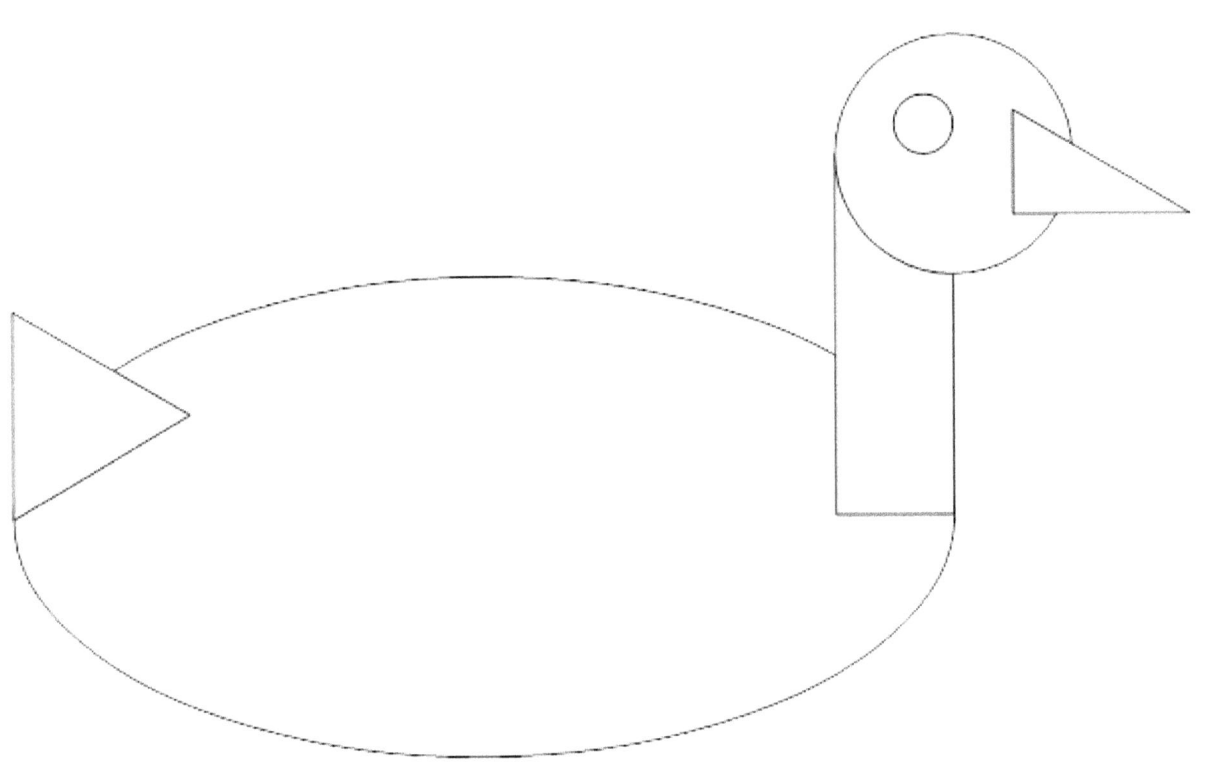

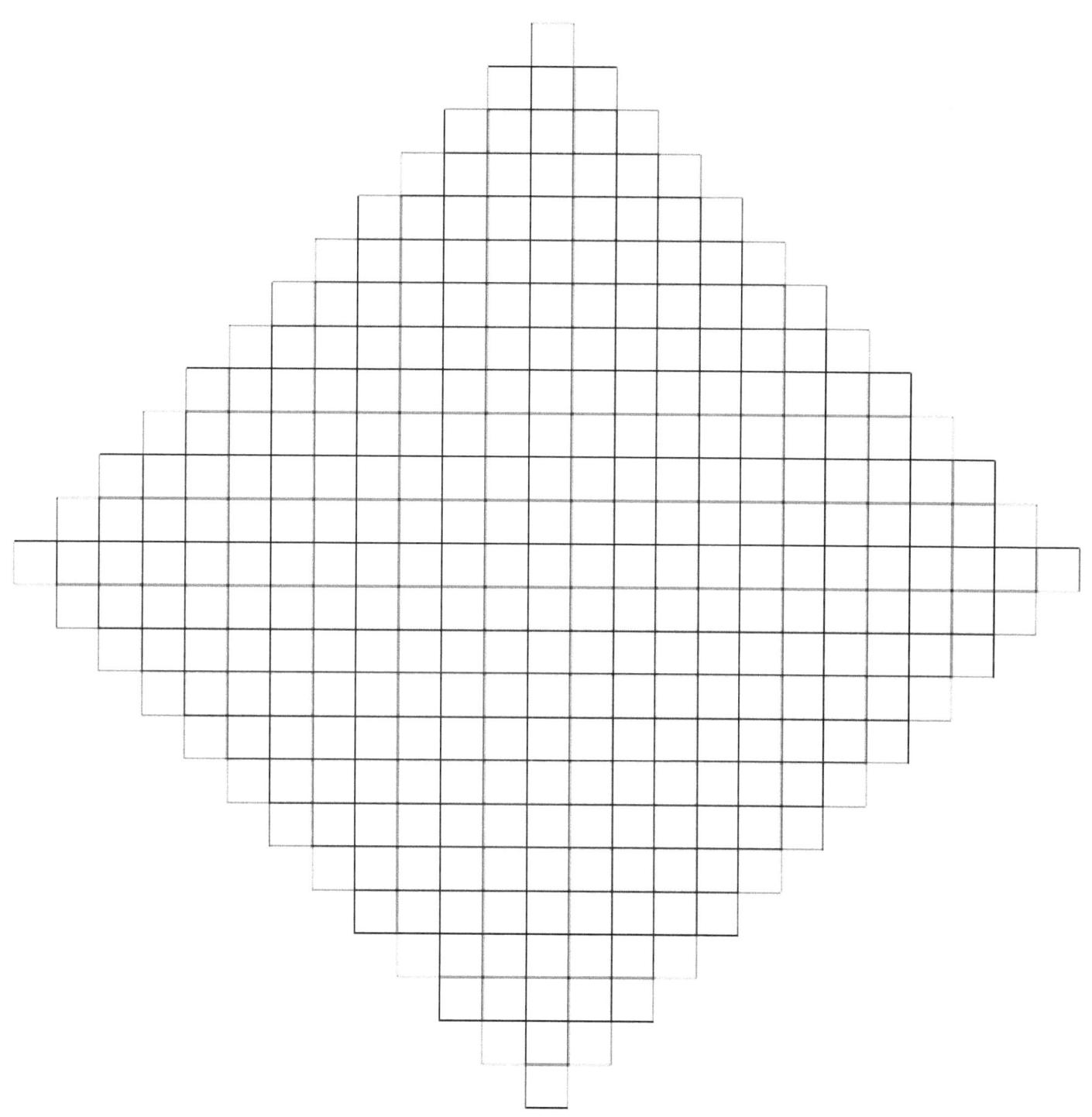

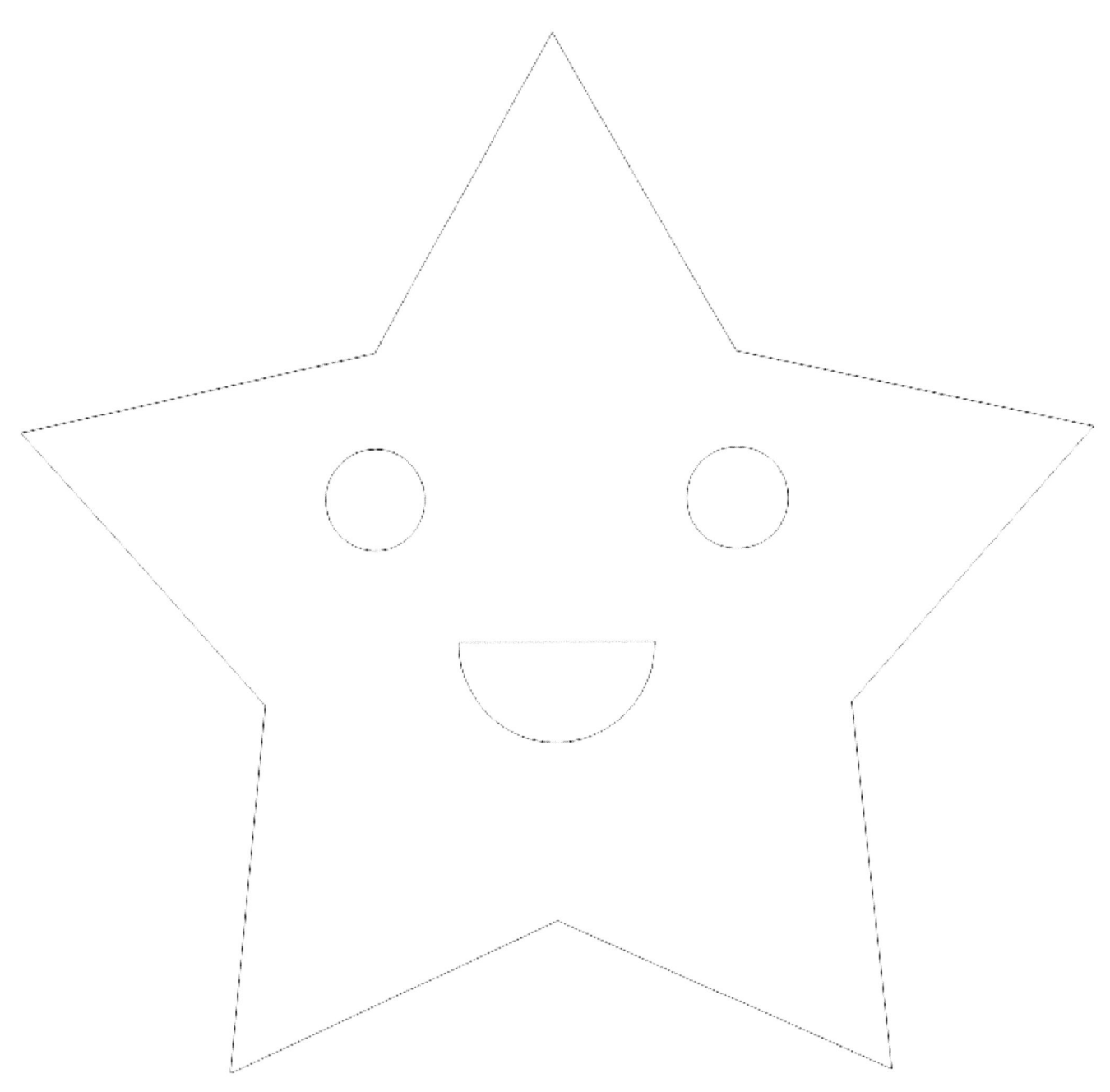

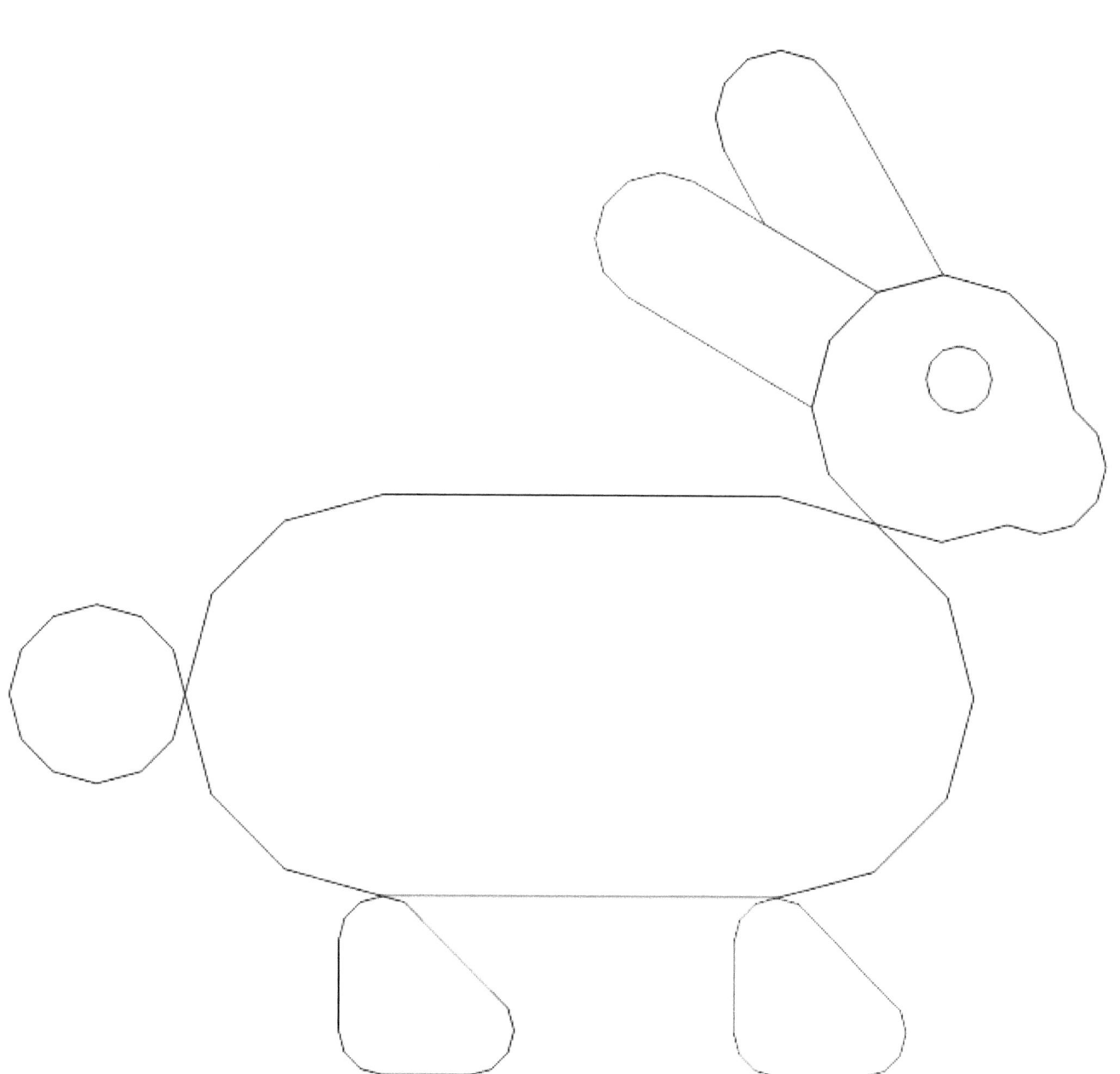

The Stories of the Animals

As I mentioned in my other art books, the horse is special to my for a variety of reasons. For this reason it tends to show up in some of my art and I often share anything horse related I find on Facebook.

The stories of the duck and the bunny are not so obvious however. The duck was something that I made after a joke by my friend Lucas while I was at his house. His dog named Tyrian was tearing up a stuffed duck and making a huge mess. Lucas said that he took away Tyrian's "duck privileges" by hiding the duck. After I made a geometric duck, I included it in my second art book.

The rabbit on the cover of this book started out because of the fact that so many people believe in the Easter bunny and it becomes a common thing in the spring to see rabbit shaped things sold in stores.

However there is a little bit more to the story. Rabbits are one of the lab animals which are continually tested on and killed regularly. If you've seen my other books you already know that I'm an ethical vegan and want the world to stop eating animals and their products so that they will no longer be in an endless cycle of breeding, torture, and death.

However there is still a lot of other cruelty when it comes to other animals such as rabbits, rats, mice, or guinea pigs which are used to test cosmetics and medications. Because rabbits are so commonly used, they have become a symbol for products labelled cruelty free and/or vegan. Rabbits are perfect for this because not only are they a cute animal which most humans would not want to cause harm to, but they themselves eat only plants and in this way are just like the horse are another example of an animal that shows humans what they should be like.

The bunny serves to remind people to consider which sources they buy their cosmetics or other things from. Killing bunnies is cruel. Period.